Bloom's Modern Critical Interpretations

Bloom's Modern Critical Interpretations

Ray Bradbury's
Fahrenheit 451
New Edition

Edited and with an introduction by
Harold Bloom
Sterling Professor of the Humanities
Yale University

BLOOM'S
LITERARY CRITICISM
An imprint of Infobase Publishing

Bloom's Modern Critical Interpretations: Fahrenheit 451—New Edition

Copyright © 2008 Infobase Publishing

Introduction © 2008 by Harold Bloom

Bloom's Literary Criticism
An imprint of Infobase Publishing
132 West 31st Street
New York NY 10001

Library of Congress Cataloging-in-Publication Data
Ray Bradbury's Fahrenheit 451, new edition / Harold Bloom. — New ed.
    p. cm. — (Bloom's modern critical interpretations)
  Includes bibliographical references and index.
  ISBN 978-1-60413-144-4 (acid-free paper) 1. Bradbury, Ray, 1920– Fahrenheit 451.
2. Science fiction, American—History and criticism. 3. Book burning in literature. I.
Bloom, Harold. II. Title: Fahrenheit 451. III. Series.

  PS3503.R167F3365 2008
  813'.54—dc22

                                    2008008776

Bloom's Literary Criticism books are available at special discounts when purchased in bulk quantities for businesses, associations, institutions, or sales promotions. Please call our Special Sales Department in New York at (212) 967-8800 or (800) 322-8755.

You can find Bloom's Literary Criticism on the World Wide Web at
http://www.chelseahouse.com

Contributing Editor: Pamela Loos
Composition by EJB Publishing Services
Cover designed by Ben Peterson
Cover printed by Yurchak Printing, Landisville, Pa.
Book printed and bound by Yurchak Printing, Landisville, Pa.
Printed in the United States of America

This book is printed on acid-free paper.

All links and Web addresses were checked and verified to be correct at the time of publication. Because of the dynamic nature of the Web, some addresses and links may have changed since publication and may no longer be valid.

Contents

Contents

Editor's Note

My slender introduction categorizes *Fahrenheit 451* as a period piece, but recognizes that Bradbury had the wit to commend memory and memorization as the true answers to bookburning.

Jack Zipes, a considerable scholar of literature and of folklore, sees Bradbury's vision of America as badly skewed and replete with contradictions, while Steven E. Kagle invokes Herman Melville as a crucial source for Bradbury.

Fahrenheit 451 is contrasted to *A Canticle for Leibowitz* by Susan Spencer who rightfully prefers Walter Miller's richer parable to Bradbury's.

Diane S. Wood juxtaposes Bradbury to Margaret Atwood's *The Handmaid's Tale*, both warnings as to the future of American society from Reagan on down.

Ray Bradbury himself writes a foreword to *Fahrenheit 451*, in which Hugh Hefner appears as savior-publisher.

The image of the mirror is expounded by Rafeeq O. McGiveron, after which Robin Anne Reid also centers upon Bradbury's image clusters.

George E. Connor examines the use of Plato's Allegory of the Cave, while Jonathan R. Eller and William F. Touponce invoke Nietzsche and Bachelard as appropriate authorities.

HAROLD BLOOM

Introduction

While *Fahrenheit 451* manifestly is a "period piece," this short, thin, rather tendentious novel has an ironic ability to inhabit somewhat diverse periods. In its origins, the book belongs to the Cold War of the 1950s, yet it prophesied aspects of the 1960s, and has not lost its relevance as I consider it in the year 2000. One does not expect the full madness of a new Theological Age to overwhelm the United States, despite hearing both George W. Bush and Albert Gore proclaim that they never make a decision without consulting Christ. And yet, in time, there may be no books to burn. In the Age of Information, how many will read Shakespeare or Dante?

I resort to a merely personal anecdote. A little while back, the New British Library wished to celebrate its grand instauration, and invited me to show up to help close a self-congratulatory week. At a Friday afternoon symposium, I was to make a third, in conjunction with the leading British authorities on software, and on "information retrieval." After I protested that I did not know what the latter was, and knew nothing of software (having not yet learned to type), I was told that my function would be to "represent books." I declined the compliment and the invitation, while reflecting gloomily that a once great library was betraying itself.

Rereading *Fahrenheit 451* after many years, I forgive the novel its stereotypes and its simplifications because of its prophetic hope that memory (and memorization!) is the answer. When I teach Shakespeare or American poetry I urge my students to read and reread *Macbeth* and *Song of Myself* over and over again, until these essential works are committed to memory. Myself, I have *eaten the books* (to employ a Talmudic trope), and I repeat poems and plays to myself for part of each day. Bradbury, a half-century ago,

1

had the foresight to see that the age of the Screen (movie, TV, computer) could destroy reading. If you cannot read Shakespeare and his peers, then you will forfeit memory, and if you cannot remember, then you will not be able to think.

Bradbury, though his work is of the surface, will survive as a moral fabulist. "The house will crumble and the books will burn," Wallace Stevens mournfully prophesied, but a saving remnant will constitute a new party of Memory. In our America-to-come, the party of Memory will become the party of Hope, a reversal of Emersonian terms, but hardly of Emersonian values. Is there a higher enterprise now than stimulating coming generations to commit to memory the best that has been written?

JACK ZIPES

Mass Degradation of Humanity and Massive Contradictions in Bradbury's Vision of America in Fahrenheit 451

Perhaps it is endemic to academic criticism of science fiction to talk in abstractions and haggle over definitions of utopia, dystopia, fantasy, science, and technology. Questions of rhetoric, semiotic codes, structure, motifs, and types take precedence over the historical context of the narrative and its sociopolitical implications. If substantive philosophical comments are made, they tend to be universal statements about humanity, art, and the destiny of the world. Such is the case with Ray Bradbury's *Fahrenheit 451*. As a result, we hear that the novel contains a criticism of "too rapid and pervasive technological change" within a tradition of "humanistic conservatism."[1] Or, it is actually "the story of Bradbury, disguised as Montag and his lifelong affair with books" and contains his major themes: "the freedom of the mind, the evocation of the past; the desire for Eden; the integrity of the individual; the allurements and traps of the future."[2] One critic has interpreted the novel as portraying a "conformist hell."[3] Another regards it as a social commentary about the present which levels a critique at "the emptiness of modern mass culture and its horrifying effects."[4]

All these interpretations are valid because they are so general and apparent, but they could also pertain to anyone or anything that lived in a "little how town." Their difficulty is that they form abstractions about figures already extrapolated from a particular moment in American history, and these

---

abstractions are not applied to the particular moment as it informs the text, but to the universe at large. Thus, *Fahrenheit 451* is discussed in terms of the world's problems at large when it is essentially bound to the reality of the early 1950s in America, and it is the specificity of the crises endangering the fabric of American society which stamp the narrative concern. The McCarthy witch hunts, the Cold War, the Korean War, the rapid rise of television as a determinant in the culture industry, the spread of advertisement, the abuse of technology within the military-industrial complex, the frustration and violence of the younger generation, the degradation of the masses[5]—these are the factors which went into the making of *Fahrenheit 451* as an American novel, and they form the parameters of any discussion of the dystopian and utopian dimensions of this work.

Bradbury is an eminently careful and conscious writer, and he always has specific occurrences and conditions in mind when he projects into the future. In *Fahrenheit 451*, he was obviously reacting to the political and intellectual climate of his times and intended to play the sci-fi game of the possible with his readers of 1953. Obviously this game is still playable in 1983 and may continue to appeal to readers in the future. It depends on the author's rhetorical ability to create a mode of discourse which allows him to exaggerate, intensify, and extend scientific, technological, and social conditions from a current real situation to their most extreme point while convincing the reader that everything which occurs in the fantasy world is feasible in the distant future. Belief in reality is at no time expected to be suspended. On the contrary, the reader is expected to bear in mind the reality of his/her situation to be able to draw comparisons and appropriate correspondences with the fictional correlates which are projections not only of the author's imagination but of the probabilities emanating from the social tendencies of the author's environment. Thus, in *Fahrenheit 451* specific American problems of the early 1950s are omnipresent and are constantly projected into the future, estranged, negated, and finally exploded in the hope that more positive values might be reborn from the ashes in phoenix-like manner. *Fahrenheit 451* is structured around fire and death as though it were necessary to conceive new rituals and customs from the ashes of an America bent on destroying itself and possibly the world. Bradbury's vision of America and Americans assumes the form of the sci-fi game of the possible because he wants it to be played out in reality. That is, the ethical utopian rigor of the book imbues the metaphorical images with a political gesture aimed at influencing the reader's conscience and subsequent behavior in society. While Bradbury obviously takes a position against the mass degradation of humanity, there are curious massive contradictions in his illumination of social tendencies which make his own position questionable. Let us try to recast the discursive mode of the narrative in light of the sociopolitical context of Bradbury's day to see what he perceived in the social tendencies of the 1950s and what alternative paths he illuminated in anticipation of possible catastrophes.

First, a word about Montag and his situation at the beginning of the novel. As a law-enforcer, Montag symbolizes those forces of repression which were executing the orders of McCarthy supporters and the conservative United States government led by General Dwight D. Eisenhower, John Foster Dulles, and J. Edgar Hoover. He is not a simple law officer but belongs to the special agency of liquidation and espionage, similar to the FBI and CIA. Moreover, he is an insider, who at thirty years of age has reached full manhood and is perhaps at his most virile stage. This is exactly why he was created and chosen by Bradbury. At thirty, as we know from real life and from numerous other novels of the twentieth century,[6] Montag is also entering a critical stage and is most susceptible to outside influences. Therefore, he is perfect for initiating the game of the possible. Montag likes his job. He gets pleasure out of burning, and his virility is closely linked to "the brass nozzle in his fists, with this great python spitting its venomous kerosene upon the world."[7] We first encounter Montag in a fit of orgasm, idealistically fulfilling his mission of purging the world of evil books. The image of book-burning, the symbolic helmet, the uniform with a salamander on the arm and a phoenix disc on his chest suggest a situation of the past, namely the Nazis, swastikas, and book-burning of the 1930s. But it is not far from the realm of possibility in the early 1950s of America that Montag as an American fireman might be pouring kerosene over books and burning them. The censorship of books which dealt with socialism, eroticism, and sexuality in the early 1950s made the extension of Montag's actions conceivable for Bradbury and his readers. Indeed, *Fahrenheit 451* begins with an acceptable statement for the silent 1950s in America which demanded a silence to all dissent: "It was a pleasure to burn" (p. 11). Here male identity is immediately associated with liquidation and destruction, with dictatorial power. Bradbury plays with the unconscious desires of the American male and extends them into the future as reality while at the same time he immediately questions that reality and machoism through Montag's misgivings.

The narrative thread of the American male vision of 1950 hangs on Montag's piecing together what has made him into the man he is at age thirty so that he can pursue a more substantial and gratifying life. This means that he must undo social entanglements, expose his understanding to the world, and burn in a different way than he does at the beginning of the narrative. His sight is our sight. His possibilities are our possibilities. His discourse with the world is ours. What he does in the future corresponds to the tasks set for us in the 1950s which may still be with us now. Though not exactly a *Bildungsroman*, *Fahrenheit 451* is a novel of development in that Montag undergoes a learning experience which lends the book its utopian impetus. Let us consider the main stages of Montag's learning experiences because they constitute Bradbury's angry critique of America—and here we must remember that Bradbury was writing about the same time as the Angry Young Generation in England and the Beat Generation in America, groups of writers who rejected the affluence and vacuousness of technological innovation in capitalist societies.

The first phase of Montag's learning experience is initiated by Clarisse McClellan, who makes him wonder why people talk and why he does not pay attention to small things. The name Clarisse suggests light, clarity, and illumination, and Montag must be enlightened. His own ability to discuss, see, feel, and hear has been muted. He is unconscious of his own history and the forces acting on him. Clarisse infers that his consciousness has been stunted by the two-hundred-foot-long billboards, the parlour walls, races, and fun parks, all of which she avoids because they prevent her from being alone with her own thoughts. Thus, she illuminates the way Montag must take not only for his own self-questioning but for the reader's own questioning of the consciousness industry in America. Bradbury wants to get at the roots of American conformity and immediately points a finger at the complicity of state and industry for using technology to produce television programs, gambling sports games, amusement parks, and advertising to block self-reflection and blank out the potential for alternative ways of living which do not conform to fixed national standards. As Bradbury's mouthpiece, Clarisse wonders whether Montag is actually happy leading a death-in-life, and Montag quickly realizes that he is not happy when he enters his sterile and fully automatic house. He proceeds to the room where his wife Mildred is ostensibly sleeping and senses that "the room was cold but nonetheless he felt he could not breathe. He did not wish to open the curtains and open the french windows, for he did not want the moon to come into the room. So, with the feeling of a man who will die in the next hour for lack of air, he felt his way toward his open, separate, and therefore cold bed" (p. 19). The image of death is fully impressed upon him when he becomes aware that his wife has attempted suicide. This is startling, but what is even more startling for Montag is the mechanical, indifferent way the operators treat his wife with a machine that revives her by pumping new blood into her system. Moreover, he becomes highly disturbed when the pill given to his wife by the operators makes her unaware the next morning that she had tried to take her own life. Montag witnesses—because Clarisse has made him more sensitive—the manner in which technology is being used even in the field of medicine to deaden the senses while keeping people alive as machines. He is part of the deadening process. In fact, dead himself he now begins to rise from the ashes like the phoenix. He is testing wings which he never thought he had.

Clarisse is his first teacher, the one who teaches him how to fly. For one intensive week he meets with Clarisse, who instructs him through her own insight and experience why and how the alleged antisocial and disturbed people may have a higher regard for society and be more sane than those who declare themselves normal and uphold the American way of life. Bradbury attacks the American educational system through Clarisse's description of classes in school which are centered on mass media and sports and prevent critical discussion. Schooling is meant to exhaust the young so that they are tame, but the frustration felt by the young is then expressed in their "fun" outside the school, which always turns to violence. Communication gives way to games of beating up people, destroying things, and playing games like chicken. Clarisse admits that she is "'afraid of children my own age. They kill each other. Did it always used to be that way? My uncle says no. Six of my friends have been shot in the last year alone. Ten of them died in car wrecks. I'm afraid of them and they don't like me because I'm afraid'" (pp. 35–36). But it is not simply fear that cannot be shown in public but all kinds of feelings. Form has subsumed emotions and substance, dissipated humanity, so that the medium has become the message. Art has become abstract, and people are identified with the things they own. They themselves are to be purchased, used, and disposed of in an automatic way.

Montag's life was in the process of becoming a permanent fixture in a system of degradation, but it was fortunately upset by Clarisse for a week. And she upsets it again by disappearing. Despite her disappearance, she has already served an important purpose because Montag is now somewhat more capable of learning from his own experiences, and he moves into his second phase. Significantly it begins with his entering the firehouse where he will start doubting his profession. The mood is set by the firemen playing cards in the tidy, polished firehouse, idling away the time until they can destroy, and the "radio hummed somewhere ... war may be declared any hour. This country stands ready to defend its—" (p. 38). Throughout the novel, war lurks in the background until it finally erupts. The obvious reference here is to the Cold War and the Korean War which might lead to such an atomic explosion as that which occurs at the end of the book. Again the media spread one-sided news about the nation's cause, driving the people hysterically to war instead of convincing them to seek means for communication and co-existence.

Montag gradually learns how the government manipulates the masses through the media, shows of force, and legal measures to pursue its own ends. His first lesson is quick and simple when he discusses a man who was obviously sane but was taken to an insane asylum because he had been reading books and had built his own library. Captain Beatty remarks: "'Any man's insane who thinks he can fool the Government and us'" (p. 39). Montag's next lesson comes from his direct experience of witnessing a woman destroy herself because her books are burned by the firemen. This incident causes Montag to bring a book back to his own house and to question what it is in books that would make a woman want to stay in a burning house. For the first time in his life he realizes that human effort and feelings go into the making of a book, and he resolves, despite a warning visit from Beatty, to pursue an experiment with his wife so that they can understand why their lives are in such a mess. Beatty had already attempted to give a false historical explanation of how firemen had been organized by Benjamin Franklin to burn English-influenced books. This time he tries a different ploy by placing the responsibility on the people and arguing that the different ethnic minority and interest groups did not want controversial subjects aired in books. This led to vapid and insipid publications. "'But the public, knowing what it wanted, spinning happily, let the comic-books survive. And the three-dimensional sex magazines, of course. There you have it, Montag. It didn't come from the Government down. There was no dictum, no declaration, no censorship, to start with, no! Technology, mass exploitation, and minority pressure carried the trick, thank God. Today, thanks to them, you can stay happy all the time, you are allowed to read comics, the good old confessions, or trade-journals'" (p. 61).

Thus, in Beatty's view—one which, incidentally is never contradicted by Bradbury—the firemen are keepers of peace. He cynically argues that the profession of firemen had to expand to keep the people happy and satisfy their complaints. This is why it conducts espionage and has a computerized system to keep track of each and every citizen in the United States. Yet, despite Beatty's explanation, Montag is firm in his resolution, for he suspects that there is more to Beatty's analysis than meets the eye. Intuitively he recalls Clarisse's discussion about her uncle and the front porches which were eliminated from people's homes because the architects (i.e., the government) did not want people to be active, talking, and communicating with one another. This is why it has become so important for him to talk to his wife and share the experiment in reading with her. However, she has been too conditioned by the television parlour games and by the seashell in her ear—the electronic waves which broadcast music and programs to prevent her thinking. Therefore, Montag is now forced to seek help from Faber, a retired English professor, who had been dismissed from the last liberal arts college because the humanities had in effect been dismissed from the educational system.

By establishing contact with Faber, whose name connotes maker or builder, Montag enters into his third stage of learning experience and begins to assume command of his own destiny. Faber teaches him that the alienation and conformity in society have not been caused by machines but by human beings who have stopped reading of their own accord, and that too few resisted the trend toward standardization and degradation of humanity—including himself. However, Montag gives him hope and courage. So he decides to begin subversive activities with a printer and to set up a communication system with Montag which will depend on the fireman's initiative. He gives Montag a green bullet through which they can communicate and plan their activities without being observed. Here technology is employed to further emancipatory and humanistic interests. The green bullet will also allow Faber to share his knowledge with Montag so that the latter will begin to think for himself. After a violent outburst at home which he knows will end his relationship with Mildred for good, Montag knows that he has made a complete rupture with his former life and recognizes the significance of his relationship with Faber. "On the way downtown he was so completely alone with his terrible error that he felt the necessity for the strange warmness and goodness that came from a familiar and gentle voice speaking in the night. Already, in a few short hours, it seemed that he had known Faber a lifetime. Now he knew that he was two people, that he was above all Montag, who knew nothing, who did not even know himself a fool, but only suspected it. And he knew also that he was the old man who talked to him and talked to him as the train was sucked from one end of the night city to the other one on a long sickening gasp of motion" (pp. 101–2). From this point on Montag moves toward regaining touch with his innermost needs and desires, and he will not be sucked into anything. He avoids the trap set for him by Beatty and burns his real enemies for the first time. His flight from the claws of the mechanical hound, which represents all the imaginative technological skills of American society transformed into a ruthless monster and used to obliterate dissenting humanity, is like the flight of the phoenix born again. Not only is Montag a new person, but he also invigorates Faber, who feels alive for the first time in years. It is a period of war on all fronts, a period of destruction and negation which is reflective of the Cold War, the Korean War, and the oppressive political climate of the 1950s. Yet, there are signs that a new, more humane world might develop after the turmoil ends.

Montag's last phase of learning is a spiritual coming into his own. He escapes to the outside world and follows the abandoned railroad track which leads him to a man whose name, Granger, indicates that he is a shepherd. Granger takes him to the collective of rebels, who are largely intellectuals. Here Bradbury suggests—as he does in many of his works—that the anti-intellectual strain in America forces most intellectuals to take an outsider position from which it is difficult to influence people. The tendency in America is to drive forward without a humanistic intellectual core.[8] Still, Montag learns that certain intellectuals have not abandoned the struggle to assert themselves and still want to assume a responsible role *within* society. Granger informs him:

> All we want to do is keep the knowledge we think we will need, intact and safe. We're not out to incite or anger anyone yet. For

if we are destroyed, the knowledge is dead, perhaps for good. We are model citizens, in our own special way; we walk the old tracks, we lie in the hills at night, and the city people let us be. We're stopped and searched occasionally, but there's nothing on our persons to incriminate us. The organization is flexible, very loose, and fragmentary. Some of us have had plastic surgery on our faces and fingerprints. Right now we have a horrible job; we're waiting for the war to begin and, as quickly, end. It's not pleasant, but then we're not in control, we're the odd minority crying in the wilderness. When the war's over, perhaps we can be of some use in the world. (p. 146)

By the end of his adventures, there is very little that Montag can learn from his mentors anymore. That is, he will undoubtedly continue to share their knowledge, but he, too, has become an imparter of knowledge. He takes the world into himself and becomes at one with it. The notions of the Book of Ecclesiastes are carried by him, and he will spread its humanistic message to help heal the rifts in the world. There is a suggestion at the end of the novel that the American society is largely responsible for the wars and destruction brought upon itself. A time has come, a season, Montag envisions, for building up. He is no longer a fireman but a prophet of humanity. The dystopian critique gives way to a utopian vision.

In their book on science fiction, Robert Scholes and Eric Rabkin state that "dystopian fiction always reduces the world to a 'State,' and presents us with the struggles of an individual or a small group against that State."[9] Later they amplify this statement by maintaining that "most twentieth-century writers have seen no way to get beyond the enslavement of technology, and we thus find a series of distinguished dystopias (like Huxley's *Brave New World*, 1932) that predict a dismal future for humanity. Some writers, however, have tried to get beyond this doom by postulating psychic growth or an evolutionary breakthrough to a race of superpeople. These tactics, of course, presume the possibility of a basic change in human nature; they do not so much see a way beyond technology as around it."[10] In *Fahrenheit 451*, Bradbury depicts the struggle of the individual against the state, or individualism versus conformity. In the process, despite the overwhelming powers of state control through mass media and technology, he has his hero Montag undergo a process of rehumanization. That is, Montag must shed the influences of the state's monopoly of the consciousness industry and regain touch with his humanistic impulse. In this regard, Bradbury follows the postulates of dystopian fiction as outlined by Scholes and Rabkin. However, there is a curious twist to the "humanistic" impulse of Bradbury which accounts for great contradictions and quasi-elitist notions of culture in *Fahrenheit 451*.

Bradbury does not locate the source of destruction in the state, class society, or technology, but in humankind itself. He has remarked that "machines themselves are empty gloves. And the hand that fills them can be good or evil. Today we stand on the rim of space, and man, in his immense tidal motion, is about to flow out toward far new worlds ... but he must conquer the seed of his own self-destruction. Man is half-idealist, half-destroyer, and the real and terrible fear is that he can still destroy himself before reaching for the stars. I see man's self-destructive half, the blind spider fiddling in the venomous dark, dreaming mushroom-cloud dreams. Death solves all, it whispers, shaking a handful of atoms like a necklace of dark beads."[11] This is all rather poetic and virtuous, but it is also naive and simplistic because Bradbury, while recognizing the awesome power and tentacles of the state in *Fahrenheit 451*, shifts the blame for the rise of totalitarianism and technological determination onto man's "nature," as if there were something inherent in the constitution of humankind which predetermines the drives, wants, and needs of the masses. Both Beatty and Faber serve as Bradbury's mouthpiece here, and they depict a history in which the masses are portrayed as ignorant, greedy, and more interested in the comfort provided by technology than in creativity and humanistic communication. As we know, Beatty maintains that the different ethnic and minority groups had become offended by the negative fashion in which the mass media depicted them. Thus the machines and the mass media were compelled to eliminate differences and originality. The mass strivings of all these different groups needed more and more regulation and standardization by the state. Thus, individualism, uniqueness, and a critical spirit had to be phased out of the socialization process. Books had to be banned, and the mass media had to be employed to prevent human beings from critical deliberation and reflection.

This analysis exonerates the state and private industry from crimes against humanity and places the blame for destructive tendencies in American society on the masses of people who allegedly want to consume and lead lives of leisure dependent on machine technology. Bradbury portrays such an existence as living death, and only intellectuals or book-readers are capable of retaining their humanity because they have refused to comply with the pressures of "democracy" and the masses who have approved of the way in which the state uses technological control and provides cultural amusement. Faber makes this point even clearer than Beatty: "'The whole culture's shot through. The skeleton needs melting and reshaping. Good God, it isn't as simple as just picking up a book you laid down half a century ago. Remember, the firemen are rarely necessary. The public itself stopped reading of its own accord'" (p. 87). Faber equates human beings with "squirrels" racing about cages (p. 87) and calls them the "solid unmoving cattle of the majority" (p. 107).

The dystopian constellation of conflict in *Fahrenheit 451* is not really constituted by the individual versus the state, but the intellectual versus the masses. The result is that, while Bradbury does amply reflect the means and ways the state endeavors to manipulate and discipline its citizens in the United States, he implies that the people, i.e., the masses, have brought this upon themselves and almost deserve to be blown up so that a new breed of book-lovers may begin to populate the world. (This is also suggested in *The Martian Chronicles* and such stories as "Bright Phoenix.") This elitist notion ultimately defeats the humanistic impulse in Bradbury's critique of mass technology and totalitarianism because he does not differentiate between social classes and their vested interests in America, nor can he explain or demonstrate from a political perspective—and essentially all utopian and dystopian literature is political—who profits by keeping people enthralled and unconscious of the vested power interests.

True, the quality of culture and life in the America of the 1950s had become impoverished, and machines loomed as an awesome threat since a military-industrial complex had been built during World War II and threatened to instrumentalize the lives of the populace. Nor has the quality been improved, or the threat diminished. But this deplorable situation is not due, as Bradbury would have us believe, to the "democratic" drives and wishes of the masses. Such basic critiques of society and technology as Herbert Marcuse's *One-Dimensional Man*, William Leiss's *The Domination of Nature*, and Harry Braverman's *Labor and Monopoly Capital* have shown that mass conformity has its roots in relations of private property and capital, not in the "nature" of humankind. In particular, Braverman provides an apt analysis of the degradation of work and life in the twentieth century. He focuses clearly on the problem which concerns Bradbury, yet which is distorted in the dystopian projection of *Fahrenheit 451*:

> The mass of humanity is subjected to the labor process for the purposes of those who control it rather than for any general purposes of 'humanity' as such. In thus acquiring concrete form, the control of humans over the labor process turns into its opposite and becomes the control of the labor process over the mass of humans. Machinery comes into the world not as the servant of 'humanity,' but as the instrument of those to whom the accumulation of capital gives the *ownership* of the machines. The capacity of humans to control the labor process through machinery is seized upon by management from the beginning of capitalism as the *prime means whereby production may be controlled not by the direct producer but by the owners and representatives of capital*. Thus, in addition to its technical function of increasing the

productivity of labor—which would be a mark of machinery under any social system—machinery also has in the capitalist system the function of divesting the mass of workers of their control over their own labor. It is ironic that this feat is accomplished by taking advantage of the great human advance represented by the technical and scientific developments that increase human control over the labor process. It is even more ironic that this appears perfectly 'natural' to the minds of those who, subjected to two centuries of this fetishism of capital, actually see the machine as an alien force which subjugates humanity.[12]

It might be argued that Bradbury has no sense of irony. Certainly his depiction of conformity and neo-fascism in America lacks subtle mediations, and thus the potential of his utopian vision wanes pale at the end of *Fahrenheit 451*. In fact, it is debatable whether one can call his ending utopian since it is regressive—it almost yearns for the restoration of a Christian world order built on good old American front porches. A group of intellectuals who memorize books are to serve as the foundation for a new society. There is a notion here which borders on selective breeding through the cultivation of brains. Moreover, it appears that the real possibility for future development is not in human potential but in the potential of books. That is, the real hero of *Fahrenheit 451* is not Montag but literature. This accounts for a certain abstract dehumanization of the characters in Bradbury's novel: they function as figures in a formula. They are sketchily drawn and have less character than the implied integrity of books. In essence, Bradbury would prefer to have a world peopled by books rather than by humans.

This becomes even more clear when we regard François Truffaut's film adaptation of *Fahrenheit 451*. Truffaut maintained that

the theme of the film is the love of books. For some this love is intellectual: you love a book for its contents, for what is written inside it. For others it is an emotional attachment to the book as an object. . . . On a less individual and intimate level, the story interests me because it is a reality: the burning of books, the persecution of ideas, the terror of new concepts, these are elements that return again and again in the history of mankind. . . . In our society, books are not burnt by Hitler or the Holy Inquisition, they are rendered useless, drowned in a flood of images, sounds, objects. And the intellectuals, the real ones, the honest ones, are like Jews, like the Resistance; if you're a thinker in the world of objects, you're a heretic; if you're different, you're an enemy. A person who creates a crisis in society because he acknowledges his bad conscience—the living proof that not everyone has betrayed in exchange for a country house, for a car, or for a collection of electronic gadgets—he is a man to eliminate along with his books.[13]

Though Truffaut's interpretation of Bradbury's novel is informed by his French consciousness and experience of fascism and the Resistance, he extends the basic theme of the novel to its most logical, universal conclusion. From the very beginning of the film, the heroes are the books themselves, and all of Truffaut's changes highlight the significance of the books. For instance they are always prominent in each frame in which they appear, and the characters are dwarfed by them in comparison. The people are less human, sexual, and alive than in Bradbury's novel. The divisions between good and evil become blurred so that all human beings without distinction share in the guilt for the mass degradation of humanity. The same actress plays Clarisse and Mildred; Montag becomes more ambivalent as a moral protagonist while his adversary Beatty becomes more sympathetic. The defenders of the books are not noble creatures, and, even in the last frame where people actually become books themselves, they are less significant than the literature and do not seem capable of communication. Annette Insdorf has pointed out that

> Truffaut's film explores the power of the word—but as a visual more than an oral entity. In a sense, the main characters are the books themselves. Truffaut even noted that he could not allow the books to fall out of the frame: "I must accompany their fall to the ground. The books here are characters, and to cut their passage would be like leaving out of frame the head of an actor." During the book-burning, close-ups of pages slowly curling into ashes look almost like fists of defiance. As in *The Soft Skin*, he suggests that the written word can capture and convey emotional depths, while the spoken is doomed to skim surfaces. The stylistic analogue to this sentiment can be found in the film's subordination of the dialogue to visual expression.[14]

While it is true that both Bradbury and Truffaut desire to show that behind each book there is a human being, their obsession with books and literature leads them away from exploring the creative potential of people themselves, who are portrayed both in the novel and film as easily manipulated and devoid of integrity. In the film, the settings and costumes are both futuristic and contemporary, and they evoke a suburban, anonymous atmosphere. Conformity is the rule, and the landscape is frozen and sterile.

Strange as it may seem, the book-lovers or exiles do not seem capable of breaking through the homogenized barren setting and congealed human relations. Again, this is due to Truffaut's adherence to the basic assumptions of Bradbury's critique, which retains its elitist notions and can only display frustration and contradictions. What is lacking in both novel and film is a more comprehensive grasp of the forces which degrade humanity and the value of literature. The dystopian constellation does not illuminate the path for resistance or alternatives because it obfuscates the machinations of the power relations of state and private industry which hinder humans from coming into their own. Bradbury in particular exhibits no faith in the masses while trying to defend humanity, and the dystopia which he constructs does not shed light on concrete utopian possibilities.

In Ernst Bloch's study of concrete utopias reflected by literature, he discusses the important notion of *Vor–Schein*, or anticipatory illumination, which is crucial for judging the social value of the imaginative conception. The symbols and chiffres of a literary work must illuminate the tendencies of reality and at the same time anticipate the potential within reality if they are seriously concerned with projecting the possibility for realizing concrete utopias, those brief moments in history such as the French Revolution, the Paris Commune, the October Revolution in Russia, etc., when actual models for egalitarian government and non-exploitative social relations were allowed to take form. The latent possibilities for such concrete utopias must be made apparent through the work of art, and their truth value depends on whether the artist perceives and captures the tendencies of the times. In discussing Bloch's philosophical categories and their significance for science fiction, Darko Suvin discusses anticipatory illumination in terms of the novum, "the totalizing phenomenon or relationship deviating from the author's and implied reader's norm of reality."[15] Suvin maintains that "the most important consequence of an understanding of SF as a symbolic system centered on a novum which is to be cognitively validated within the narrative reality of the tale and its interaction with reader expectations is that the novelty has to be convincingly explained in concrete, even if imaginary terms, that is, in terms of the *specific* time, place, agents, and cosmic and social totality of each tale."[16]

Like Bloch, Suvin uses this notion of novum to clarify the political and ethical function of utopian literature. The artistic depiction of social tendencies and the novum always indicates willy-nilly the actual possibilities for putting into practice new and alternative forms of human comportment which might enable humankind to emancipate itself from alienating and oppressive conditions. Bloch regards both life and art as a process with utopia serving as a beacon, illuminating those elements and moments which can bring to life what-has-not-been-realized:

The lonely island, where utopia is supposed to lie, may be an archetype. However, it creates a stronger effect through ideal figures of a sought-after perfection, as free or ordered development of the contents of life. That is, the utopian function should essentially hold to the same line as the utopias themselves: the line of concrete mediation with an ideal tendency rooted in the material world, as mentioned before. In no way can the ideal be taught and reported through mere facts. On the contrary, its essence depends on its strained relationship to that which has become merely factual. If the ideal is worth anything, then it has a connection to the process of the world, in which the so-called facts are reified and fixed abstractions. The ideal has in its anticipations, if they are concrete, a correlate in the objective contents of hope belonging to the latent tendency. This correlate allows for *ethical ideals as models, aesthetic ones as anticipatory illuminations which point to the possibility of becoming real.* Such ideals which are reported and delivered through a utopian function are then considered altogether as the content of a humanely adequate, fully developed self and world. Therefore, they are—what may here be considered in the last analysis as a summary or simplification of all ideal existence—collectively inflexions of the basic content—the most precious thing on earth.[17]

Though Bradbury is idealistic, ethical, and highly critical of reified conditions in the America of the 1950s, the utopian function in *Fahrenheit 451* is predicated on a false inflexion of tendencies and contradictions in American society. The novum is not a true novelty allowing for qualitatively changed human relationships and social relations. Montag's learning experience reflects Bradbury's confused understanding of state control, education, private industry, and exploitative use of the mass media. Since he does not dig beneath the people and facts as they are, he cannot find the utopian correlate which points to realizable possibilities in the future. It is a far-fetched dream to have book-lovers and intellectuals as the progenitors of a new society, especially when they have an inaccurate notion of what led the "bad old" society to become fascist and militaristic. The ethical and aesthetic ideals in Bradbury's narrative are derived from an indiscriminate and eclectic praise of books per se. Despite his humanitarian intentions, Bradbury's hatred for the machine and consumer age, its effect on the masses, and the growing deterioration of the cultural level through the mass media led him to formulate romantic anticapitalist notions from an elitist point of view. Thus, what becomes significant about Bradbury's attempt to depict utopian possibilities for humankind individualized like a phoenix rising from the fire is his own contradictory relationship to America.

There is an acute tension between the intellectual and the majority of people in America. There is a disturbing element in the manner by which dissent and doubt are often buried in standard patriotic rhetoric in America. Yet, there are just as many intellectuals and book-lovers, often called mandarins, who upheld the formation of the military-industrial complex in the 1940s and 1950s, as there are those who dissented.[18] To love a book or to be an intellectual is not, as Bradbury would have us believe, ideally ethical and humane. Writing at a time when the military-industrial complex was being developed and received the full support of the university system, Bradbury overlooked the interests of private corporations and complicitous network of intellectuals and book-lovers who have created greater instrumental control of the masses. Such an oversight short-circuits the utopian function of his books, and he remains blind to the intricacies of control in his own society. Books are not being burned with "1984" around the corner. Books are proliferating and being distributed on a massive scale. They are being received and used in manifold ways just as are the mass media such as television, film, radio, video—and not by a solid mass of cattle. The struggles of minority groups and women for equal rights and alternate technology and ecology point to certain massive contradictions which underlie the premise of *Fahrenheit 451*. If there is a utopian vision in Bradbury's novel, then it is based on a strange love of humanity and will surely never be concretized unless by books themselves.

NOTES

1. A. James Stupple, "The Past, The Future, and Ray Bradbury," in *Voices for The Future*, ed. Thomas D. Clareson (Bowling Green: Bowling Green Univ. Popular Pr., 1976), p. 24.

2. Willis E. McNelly, "Ray Bradbury—Past, Present, and Future," in *Voices for The Future*, pp. 169, 173.

3. Kingsley Amis, *New Maps of Hell* (New York: Harcourt, Brace, 1960), p. 110.

4. Joseph Blakey, *Fahrenheit 451* (Toronto: 1972), Coles Notes, pp. 90–91.

5. For good background material on this period, see Daniel Snowman, *America Since 1920* (New York: Harper and Row, 1968); I. F. Stone, *The Haunted Fifties* (London: Merlin, 1964); and Howard Zinn, *Postwar America* (Indianapolis: Bobbs-Merrill, 1973).

6. See Theodore Ziolkowski, *Fictional Transfigurations of Jesus* (Princeton: Princeton Univ. Pr., 1972). Like Jesus Christ, who went out preaching at age thirty, Montag has features of a Christ figure.

7. *Fahrenheit 451* (1953 rpt. London: Panther Books, 1976), p. 11. Hereafter all quotations cited in the text shall be taken from this volume.

8. See Richard Hofstadter, *Anti-intellectualism in American Life* (New York: Knopf, 1963).

9. *Science Fiction: History, Science, Vision* (London: Oxford Univ. Pr., 1977), p. 34.

10. Ibid., p. 174.

11. Quoted in William F. Nolan, "Bradbury: Prose Poet in the Age of Space," *Fantasy and Science Fiction* 24 (May 1963): 8. For similar statements by Bradbury, see *The Ray Bradbury Companion*, ed., William F. Nolan (Detroit: Gale Research, 1975), and the special Ray Bradbury issue of *Rocket's Blast—Comicollector*, vol. 131 (Oct. 1976), pp. 14–17, 28–29.

12. *Labor and Monopoly Capital* (New York: Monthly Review Pr., 1974), p. 193.

13. Quoted in C. G. Crisp, *François Truffaut* (New York: Praeger, 1972), pp. 81–82.

14. *François Truffaut* (Boston: Twayne, 1978), p. 49.

15. *Metamorphoses of Science Fiction* (New Haven: Yale Univ. Pr., 1979), p. 64.

16. Ibid., p. 80.

17. *Ästhetik des Vor-Scheins*, vol. 1, ed. Gert Ueding (Frankfurt am Main: Suhrkamp, 1974), P. 296.

18. The best depiction of this sad history is James Ridgeway, *The Closed Corporation: American Universities in Crisis* (New York: Random House, 1968). See also G. William Domhoff, *Who Rules America?* (Englewood Cliffs, N.J.: Prentice-Hall, 1967); and Herbert I. Schiller, *Mass Communications and American Empire* (Boston: Beacon, 1971).

STEVEN E. KAGLE

Homage to Melville: Ray Bradbury and the Nineteenth-Century American Romance

When we finally try to categorize Ray Bradbury's place as a writer we will ultimately place him beside Herman Melville and Stephen King rather than Jules Verne and Arthur C. Clarke. In placing him with Melville I am not attempting to equate the quality of Bradbury's work with Melville's, only asserting that Bradbury's place in literary history is closer to that of Melville and other nineteenth-century writers of the prose romance than it is to twentieth century writers of science fiction.

Moreover, Bradbury's interest in Melville is particularly extensive and important.[1] He wrote the screenplay for John Huston's adaptation of *Moby-Dick* (released in 1956). Years later he also wrote "Leviathan 99," an hour long radio play adaptation of *Moby-Dick* put on by the BBC in 1968.

Bradbury wrote poems of some length about the creation of *Moby-Dick*. In one entitled "That Son of Richard III" he wrote about the influence of Shakespeare on *Moby-Dick*, an accurate assessment, even though in making it he perpetuated the notion, now conclusively rejected by critics, that before encountering Shakespeare's plays, Melville had been writing a very different work, an *Ur-Moby-Dick* in which Ahab did not appear:

> At first there was no captain to the ship
> Which, named Pequod,

From *The Celebration of the Fantastic*, pp. 279–289. © 1992 by Donald E. Morse, Marshall B. Tymn, and Csilla Bertha.

Set sail for destinations, not for God.
But: God obtruded, rose and blew his breath
And Ahab rose, full born, to follow Death,
Know dark opinions,
Seek in strangest salt dominions for one Beast. . . .
How came it so? . . .
Why Willie happened by!
That is the end, explanation, and the all. . . .
Shakespeare beneath his window gave his shout:
"Oh Lazarus! Herman Melville! truly come ye forth!
And what's with you?
Dreadful gossamer?
Funeral wake or Arctic veil?"
"What's this? Why, Jesus, lily-of-the-valley breath,
It seems to be . . .
A Whale!"
And what a whale! A trueborn Beast of God." *Poems* 48–9

Thus far the poem seems to be supporting a fairly common assertion that writers are inspired by other writers, leading us to the reasonably obvious judgment that as Melville was inspired by Shakespeare, so Bradbury was inspired by Melville. However, the relationships among these writers is far more complex. Later in the poem Bradbury envisions Melville reversing roles, and as Shakespeare has summoned him to creative effort, he summons Shakespeare to be reborn in the spirit of Moby-Dick:

O Lazarus William Shakespeare,
Come *you* forth in a whale!
And Will all fleshed in marble white
Could not prevail against such summonings and . . .
Was clamored forth to freedom in a Whale. (51)

Bradbury's suggestion that Melville's white whale was a personification of Shakespeare has several implications. One, of course, is that some of Bradbury's characters, themes, plots, and so forth pay similar homage to earlier writers he admired, a number of whom come from the American Renaissance and the periods just before and after it. Moby-Dick, Ahab, and Melville along with other American writers of Melville's century haunt other of Bradbury's poems in name, subject, and symbol: In the poem "N" Ahab haunts the dream of Jules Verne's Captain Nemo (*Poems* 184). The title of another says it all: "Emily Dickinson, Where Are You? Herman Melville Called Your Name in His Sleep Last Night."

Such homage suggests that Bradbury is conscious of another kind of authorial immortality beyond that which he may hope to achieve through the survival of his own writings, and this immortality is a survival in the writings of those authors who may become influenced by him. By referring or more subtly introducing elements from these earlier writers into his own works, Bradbury is asserting his place in an enduring tradition. The desire for such immortality may be prompted as much by fear as by hope. Like Melville and King, Bradbury seems to use his writings as a means of working out the dark elements of the human soul. The "dark inscrutable thing" that haunted Melville's rivers and oceans haunts Bradbury's works. As Melville noted in "Hawthorne and his Mosses," the perception of this "mystical blackness" not merely allows, but compels such artists to produce their work.

In another poem entitled "Old Ahab's Friend and Friend to Noah, Speaks His Piece," Bradbury even more fully reveals his sense of the connections among *Moby-Dick*, science fiction, and his own career:

> At night he swims within my sight
> And looms with ponderous jet within my mind
> And delves into the waves and deeps himself in dreams;
> He is and is not what he seems.
> The White Whale, stranger to my life,
> Now takes me as his writer-kin, his feeble son,
> His wifing husband, husband-wife.
> I swim with him. I dive. I go to places never seen. (160)

In Bradbury's imagination Moby-Dick, who seems the symbol of creative inspiration, addresses him and through him, mankind.

> You are the inhalation of a commencement of a beginning,
> A flowering of life that will never close. . . .
> While your soul glides, you wander on,
> You take the air with wings.
> Test fires, roar, thrash, leap upon the Universe Itself!
> And breathing, move in breathless yammerings of broadcast Space.
> Among the energies of abyss-void you bound and swim
> And take a rocket much like me
> The White Whale built out of steel and loxxed with energy
> And skinned all round with yet more metal skin. (160-1)

Moby-Dick becomes transformed for Bradbury from the symbol of all that stifles mankind, the "pasteboard mask" that keeps him from seeing the true world of the spirit, the wall that limits him, and becomes instead the symbol of liberation. Bradbury seems almost to endorse Ahab's error that "God's true worship is defiance" that, as Emerson suggested in his poem "The World Soul":

> gods delight in gods,
> And thrust the weak aside;
> To him who scorns their charities
> Their arms fly open wide.

Bradbury likes science fiction because it suggests a freedom from limits:

> I am the Ark of Life. You be the same.
> Build you a fiery whale all white,
> Give it my name.
> Ship with Leviathan for forty years
> Until an isle in Space looms up to match your dreams.
> (*Poems* 162)

This transformation of Moby-Dick into a white rocket supports the extension of the association between Bradbury and Melville from Bradbury's poems to those of his prose works that have been classified as science fiction. I say, "classified as science fiction" because, while his best known works, *The Martian Chronicles* (1950) and *Fahrenheit 451* (1953), have led the general public to think of Ray Bradbury as a science fiction writer, both literary critics and science fiction fans have often argued against such a classification. In an article published in the *Journal of Science Fiction*, written the year after *The Martian Chronicles* and entitled "The Case Against Ray Bradbury," Edward Wood expressed the hope that if Bradbury achieved better discipline in his writing "Some day he [might] . . . even write some science fiction" (Mogen 19).

I would not go so far; however, I would agree that Bradbury has only rarely written works that should be classified as science fiction.[2] Many of Bradbury's works like *Dandelion Wine* are mainstream fiction. *Death Is a Lonely Business* is a detective novel. Even his books entitled *R Is for Rocket* and *S Is for Space* contain stories that deal with neither rockets nor space. For example, the latter includes a story entitled "The Screaming Woman" about a man who buries his wife alive and another, "The Trolley," about the conversion of a trolley line into a bus route.

Any judgment about Bradbury's place as a science fiction writer will hinge upon one's definition of science fiction. If one chooses the popular definition, common among fans, that science fiction refers to those works that deal either with events in the future or locations beyond Earth, then one is likely to conclude that only a small number of his works fits into those categories, and for many of those the displacement of the plot into the future or outer space is the result of a few minor changes that represent no real technological breakthroughs, changes such as the huge television screens and robot mechanical hound in *Fahrenheit 451*. These works do not seem to extend as far beyond our world as the television series "Max Headroom" with its introduction set only "twenty minutes into the future."

Another definition (appearing in the most popular of the dictionaries of literary terms—one of the few that even ventures to define it) is that science fiction is "a form of fantasy in which scientific facts, as assumptions, or hypotheses form the basis, by logical extrapolation, of adventures in the future, on other planets, in other dimensions in time, or under new variants of scientific law" (Holman 481). This emphasis on the primacy of "scientific fact" and "technological truth" has been advanced by a number of writers, editors, and critics, especially those associated with what has been termed "hard" science fiction. However, Bradbury began reading before such critical standards for the genre had been developed. He grew up with the so called science fiction pulp magazines of the 1920s and 1930s, and the paradigm of their stories and illustrations was the bug-eyed monster from outer space lusting after and abducting a half-naked human woman. (Why an alien possessing a technology that enables it to cross space should want and consider it economic to pursue a human female was never addressed nor was the technology necessary for such a voyage.)

Much of the movement toward a different type of speculative fiction, science fiction for short, one that adhered to scientific truth, came as the result of the efforts of people such as John Campbell editor of *Astounding*. Campbell's point was that too much science fiction had too little connection with reality. How could one learn from a work that pretended to praise or warn us about the dangers of technology if that work seemed written by a technological illiterate? But Bradbury is not a technological illiterate; he tends to ignore technology and science as irrelevant to his purposes. One critic suggests that Bradbury is "a romantic, [and] a sentimentalist" using "rockets and robots" not as items of technology but as "extensions" of the human soul, expressions of his spirit rather than extensions of his physical power (Mogen 23). Such a judgment supports the view that Bradbury's debt to nineteenth-century American romance is greater than his debt to twentieth-century science fiction.

Bradbury chose Mars as the setting for his *Martian Chronicles* because he needed a world apart from our reality. Once writers could set their imaginary societies in unexplored portions of our own globe; consider the worlds of Homer's *Odyssey* and Shakespeare's "The Tempest." In the nineteenth century, Melville set works such as *Mardi* and *Moby-Dick* in largely unexplored regions of the Pacific; Poe set his *Narrative of Arthur*

Gordon Pym in the Antarctic. As late as the 1930s people could believe in a "Shangri La" lost in the Himalayas. But by the time Bradbury was writing it was harder to imagine such places on Earth, and when imagined they are necessarily small and circumscribed like the warren of tunnels under New York envisioned for the television program "Beauty and the Beast." Hawthorne removed many of his works temporally, setting them in a past sufficiently distant as to allow the possibility of spiritual forces; but today, even the past is better understood than it once was, and it is much easier for writers of the fantastic to find their settings on the decks of the starship *Enterprise* or in "a galaxy far far away" than in the known world.

Edgar Allan Poe in his "Sonnet on Science" complained that science had taken away the mystery and magic that the poet needed for his art. As part of his indictment of science, Poe complained that it had taken the moon, once thought to be the chariot of the goddess Diana, and "dragged Diana from her car." Later, science fiction writers had tried to invest the moon with new mystery, peopling it with strange alien creatures, but over a decade ago the Apollo project showed it to be a ball of dead, dusty, gray rock. Bradbury's Mars was not the real fourth planet, but it did require a suspension of disbelief. (The unmanned Mars lander started the demythification of Mars and the manned expeditions being planned by the Soviet Union and the United States are sure to complete the process.)

Bradbury's speculative fiction allows this suspension of disbelief because it is not science fiction but science fantasy, a form that lies between science fiction and fantasy. In *The Other Side of Realism*, Thomas Clareson argued that science fiction is a relatively modern form that has its roots in the "realistic" novel. Science fantasy has its roots in another type of long prose fiction (one often considered a type of novel), the prose romance. Nathaniel Hawthorne in his preface to *The House of the Seven Gables* tried to distinguish the romance and the novel by claiming that the novel aims "at a very minute fidelity, not merely to the possible, but to the probable and ordinary course of man's experience," while the romance need only be faithful to "the truth of the human heart," a truth that may include spiritual and mystical truths, its other details remaining totally subject to the author's choice (1).

The romance both in its prose and poetry forms is a much older form than the novel. The novel does have older roots, but its origins are not much older that the seventeenth century. There were three reasons for the development of the novel at that time: the invention of movable type, the rise of the middle class, and the Protestant Reformation. The first brought down the price of printed works, the second created a class with an interest in the experiences of ordinary people and the money to buy books that described such experiences; and the third, by insisting that people should interpret the Bible for themselves, fostered the literacy necessary to read literature.

Science fiction is related to the realistic tradition that produced the novel. While the futuristic settings and alien creatures that it often uses make it seem a fanciful form, true works of science fiction make only a limited number of departures from the world as we know it. Asimov's *The Foundation Series*, for example, was patterned after those of European history. The work begins at the time of the decline of a galactic empire in the distant future; yet, the events that accompany the decline and fall of that empire and the rise of the new society that takes its place are like those that occurred during the decline and fall of the Roman Empire and the rise of modern Europe from its ashes. Asimov's characters behave as humans behave; their attempts at heroism are generally the result of mere human strengths and their weaknesses are like those that we can see around us today. Even though Asimov takes the license to imagine that some individuals develop extrasensory powers, those powers are defined and limited. They only violate the laws of our world in accordance with the premises Asimov established for them.

Bradbury's speculative fiction does not attempt to adhere to either the scientific or psychological laws of our world. For example, in the section from the *Martian Chronicles* originally published under the title "Mars Is Heaven," the Martians use telepathic projection to deceive the explorers from Earth into thinking that the beings they see are dead friends and relatives from Earth resurrected on a new planet. The Martians use this deception to lull the Earthmen into a sense of security so that they can be murdered. Even if we ignore departures from scientific truth, such as an Earth-like environment on Mars, we must confront other serious problems. For example, while Bradbury tells his readers how the Martians do what they do, he seems less disposed to explain why they commit these murders, why they choose such an elaborate method to do so, or why they maintain their ruse after the Earthmen are dead. Bradbury's readers do not question these lapses, and one reason they do not is because Bradbury is such a good story teller that readers willingly suspend disbelief. However, another reason is that while the tale violates the requirements of realistic fiction and science fiction, they satisfy Hawthorne's requirement for good romance; they adhere to "the truth of the human heart."

Another example of Bradbury's ability to make his readers not merely suspend disbelief but to enter into a work controlled by new standards of belief is "The Veldt." In this story, two children murder their parents, who have planned to disconnect the machine that allows their nursery to project scenes on its walls and ceiling, making them appear to be different settings in which the children can act out their play fantasies. As the parents explain, the images on the walls are not real: "Walls . . . crystal walls, that's all they are. Oh they look real . . . but it's all dimensional superactionary supersensitive color film and mental tape behind glass screens. It's all odorphonics and sonics"

(*Illustrated Man* 17). Yet, the children are able to commit their murder by locking their parents in the nursery and letting the images of lions on the wall kill and eat them. Bradbury tells us that the ten-year-old boy is bright and may have tinkered with the machinery, but the story does not give us any rational way that even a bright child can make a lion on a television screen into a physical manifestation. Nevertheless, we as readers do not question the scientific truth of the story any more than we question how Peter Pan can make people fly by sprinkling them with fairy dust. Incidentally, the two homicidal children who do not want their nursery turned off, who do not want to grow up, are named Peter and Wendy.

Bradbury, like Melville and Hawthorne, does not condemn technology, but rather he attacks the faith in technology that makes us believe ourselves able to ignore the world of the spirit. Tom Fury, the salesman who in *Something Wicked Comes This Way* tries to peddle his lightning rods to the citizens of Green Town as a means to protect themselves against the storm of the autumn people, may be another incarnation of Melville's "Lightning Rod Man," who tries to get people to place their faith in such protection. Similarly, Mr. Dark the leader of the autumn people may have the same origin as the title figure of Melville's *The Confidence-Man*, an incarnation of the Devil, who searches among the passengers of the riverboat "Fidele" for those he can fool into giving him their confidence. By giving their confidence to the false charities that the Confidence Man peddles, the passengers are denying the existence of evil in the world, and worse, they are denying their own responsibility for it. Worst of all, they are ignoring God's connection to it.

For Melville these issues become all-consuming questions. Ahab asks if God, as the all-powerful creator of the world as it is, is, therefore, responsible for the evil in the world:

> Is it I, God, or who, that lifts this arm? But if the great sun move not of himself; but is as an errand-boy in heaven; nor one single star revolve, but by some invisible power, how then can this one small heart beat; this one small brain think thoughts; unless God does that beating, does that thinking, does that living, and not I? . . . Look! see yon Albacore! who put it into him to chase and fang that flying-fish? Where do murderers go, man? Who's to doom, when the judge himself is dragged to the bar? (535)

Bradbury's attitude toward scientific investigation and technological progress, like Melville's toward God, is ambiguous. In his story "The Flying Machine" Bradbury writes of a man of ancient China who invents a flying machine: "Clothed in bright papers and reeds to make wings and a beautiful yellow tail" he soared "like the largest bird in a universe of birds, like a new dragon in a land of ancient dragons" (*S* 228). The flying machine is a thing of great beauty and wonder, but when the man is brought before the Emperor Yuan, his reward is to be condemned to death. As the emperor explains:

> "Here is a man who has made a certain machine. . . . [For him] it is only necessary that he create, without knowing why he has done so or what this thing will do. . . . There are times when one must lose a little beauty if one is to keep what little beauty one already has . . ." The inventor may be innocent, but if others should learn of this invention, "some other man" with an "evil face and an evil heart" might "fly in the sky and drop huge stones on the Great Wall of China." (*S* 230–31)

Bradbury may be condemning the emperor (as he does the rulers in *Fahrenheit 451*) as one who seeks to destroy and hide knowledge that may threaten his power. However, he may also be warning against those individuals who, like those scientists who have devised the elegant theories and formulas that might be used to produce weapons like the atomic bomb, without considering the uses to which their inventions might be put by the unscrupulous. A decision about Bradbury's intentions is complicated by the fact that we not only know that airplanes and bombs were eventually built—support for the argument that we can not destroy knowledge by suppressing it—but also know that these weapons were not developed until a much later period than that of Bradbury's story—support for the argument that actions to hold off technology may have a significant effect.

Many readers of *Fahrenheit 451* assume that Bradbury is warning against media technology and tyrannical governments, but as Beatty, captain of the firemen who go around burning books, explains to Montag, the organized destruction of books "didn't come from the Government down. There was no dictum, no declaration, no censorship, to start with, no! Technology, mass exploitation and minority pressure carried the trick, thank God. Today thanks to them, you can stay happy all the time" (64). Though Captain Beatty includes technology in his trinity of forces that lead to the firemen, the technology his words indict is not what we would consider modern technology, but rather the technology of the mid and late nineteenth century and early twentieth century: photography, lithography, motion pictures, and radio (61). This technology merely makes possible mass marketing. Economies of scale make publishers and producers afraid to anger minority interests. Consider what has happened with textbooks. When Texas and California set standards for textbooks, any text that did not meet the approval of both was excluded from a huge market. Until recently a small group of self-proclaimed guardians of morality and patriotism were able to exercise a veto in Texas against texts that introduced values of which they disapproved. And by controlling the Texas market they controlled what would be read in most schools in this nation.

Bradbury's real concern in *Fahrenheit 451* is not that we will become television addicts but that we already have become so anti-intellectual, so afraid of thought, that we refuse to learn and make fun of those who do learn. As Beatty explained, "the word 'intellectual'. . . became the swear word it deserved to be. You always dread the unfamiliar" (53). Bradbury shows that turning off the television sets is not an answer. It will not make us any more willing to face the unpleasant lessons of history, lessons that make us unhappy, and we all want to be happy above all things. Bradbury would remind us that those who refuse to learn from history are condemned to repeat it. Granger tells Montag that the books that they and their friends are carrying in their minds are not enough to save mankind. "Even when we had the books on hand, a long time ago, we didn't use what we got out of them. We went on insulting the dead. We went on spitting on the graves of all the poor ones who died before us" (146).

I would go further to suggest that mass media such as television and cinema may be as "subversive" of the kinds of mindlessness that Bradbury condemns as are books. Science fiction and fantasy are especially subversive forms of mass media because they reach many people who seek only escape, and educate them. The 1960's television series "Star Trek" warned against war, warned against the complacent assumption that *We* were always right and *They* were always wrong, and it did so long before it was fashionable. "M*A*S*H" was a successful television series, but only after the American public had turned against the Vietnamese War. "Star Trek" worked its subversion while the war was still widely popular. A close examination of popular science fiction in the late 1980's reveals works such as "Robo-cop" and "Max Headroom" that criticize those big corporations and their executives who were seeking profits and power at the expense of human values and were doing so under a national administration that was suggesting that the public could rely on businesses to police their own pollution, regulate their own takeoffs and landings, make their own safety checks, and set their own electricity rates. As Melville wrote in "Hawthorne and His Mosses": "In this world of lies, Truth is forced to fly like a scared white doe in the woodlands; and only by cunning glimpses will she reveal herself" (244). This truth peeps out of Bradbury's fiction, and its mode of depiction is at least as much indebted to nineteenth-century American writers such as Melville as it is to Bradbury's contemporaries or close chronological predecessors.

NOTES

1. Bradbury was not the only writer associated with science fiction to be interested in Melville's epic novel. Philip José Farmer based one novel, *The Unreasoning Mask*, on a

quotation from *Moby-Dick* and in another, *The Wind Whales of Ishmael*, traced the life of Melville's narrator after the end of *Moby-Dick*, including a series of adventures in a distant future.

2. This assertion in no way impugns Bradbury's skill as a writer, rather, it shows Bradbury's writing to better advantage by showing it as it truly is. Rex Harrison starred in "My Fair Lady" and Richard Burton in "Camelot" yet the reputation of neither is diminished by the statement that they should not really classified as singers.

WORKS CITED

Bradbury, Ray. *The Complete Poems of Ray Bradbury*. New York: Ballantine, 1982.

———. *Fahrenheit 451*. New York: Ballantine Books, 1979.

———. *The Illustrated Man*. Garden City: Doubleday & Company, 1951.

———. *S Is for Space*. Garden City: Doubleday & Company, 1966.

Clareson, Thomas D. "The Other Side of Realism" in *The Other Side of Realism*. Edited by Thomas D. Clareson. Bowling Green, OH: Bowling Green Popular Press, 1971. 1–28.

Hawthorne, Nathaniel. *House of the Seven Gables*. Vol. 2. *Centenary Edition of the Works of Nathaniel Hawthorne*, edited by Hershel Parker et al. Columbus: Ohio State University Press, 1965.

Holman, C. Hugh. *A Handbook to Literature*. New York: Odyssey Press, 1972.

Melville, Herman. "Hawthorne and His Mosses" in *Piazza Tales & Other Prose Pieces 1839–1860*. Vol. 9. *The Writings of Herman Melville*, edited by William Charvat et al.: 239–53. Evanston: Northwestern University Press, 1987.

———. *Moby-Dick*. New York: Random House, 1950.

Mogen, David. *Ray Bradbury*. Boston: Twayne Publishers, 1986.

SUSAN SPENCER

The Post-Apocalyptic Library:
Oral and Literate Culture in Fahrenheit 451
and A Canticle for Leibowitz

At the dawn of widespread literacy in fourth-century Athens, Plato appended to the end of his *Phaedrus* a story that has often been perceived as, as Jacques Derrida puts it, "an extraneous mythological fantasy" (67). Derrida argues in *Dissemination* that there is nothing extraneous about the myth at all, but rather it is an expression of an important and timely idea with which the classical Athenians were concerned. Recent orality/literacy theory, as outlined by Eric A. Havelock, Walter S. Ong, and others, would seem to back him up. The story is that of the discovery of the technology of writing, a tale that Socrates claims is traditional among the Egyptians. According to Socrates, the god Theuth invented this technology and offered it to the king of Upper Egypt as something that would "make the people of Egypt wiser and improve their memories" (*Phaedrus* 274b). But the king scorned Theuth's gift, saying:

> by reason of your tender regard for the writing that is your offspring, [you] have declared the very opposite of its true effect. If men learn this, it will implant forgetfulness in their souls; they will cease to exercise memory because they rely on that which is written, calling things to remembrance no longer from within themselves, but by means of external marks. What you have discovered is a recipe not for memory, but for reminder.

From *Extrapolation* 32, no. 4 (Winter 1991), pp. 331–342. © 1991 by Kent State University Press.

> And it is no true wisdom that you offer your disciples, but
> only its semblance, for by telling them of many things without
> teaching them you will make them seem to know much, while
> for the most part they know nothing, and as men filled, not with
> wisdom, but with the conceit of wisdom, they will be a burden
> to their fellows. (275a,b)

The remark about "telling them . . . without teaching them" is evidently
an expression of uneasiness with the idea of text as what Ong calls
"unresponsive." In *Orality and Literacy: The Technologizing of the Word*, Ong
sees one of Socrates's arguments as being "if you ask a person to explain his
or her statement, you can get an explanation; if you ask a text, you get back
nothing except the same, often stupid, words which called for your question
in the first place" (79). While this idea is so commonplace to us as to go
practically unnoticed, except when we are frustrated by a particularly opaque
text, it was new and frightening to the Greeks. According to Havelock in
"The Oral Composition of Greek Drama" (*Literate Revolution* 261–312),
the late fifth and early fourth century B.C. was a period of relatively rapid
change in literary style, as a direct result of the spread of popular literacy.
Not only was an explanatory oral framework done away with, but also
the old formulaic devices that helped oral composers keep their place and
remember what they were talking about. "Compositionally, as plays began
to be written with the expectation of being read, the composer would feel a
reduced pressure to conform to certain mnemonic rules. The invented would
be freer to prevail over the expected" (266). This, Havelock hypothesizes,
created some tension in the Greek theater—a tension that can be traced in
Aristophanes's *Frogs*, where the more conservative, more "oral" Aeschylus
wins a contest against the more "literary" and startlingly original Euripides;
and, as we can see (although Havelock does not mention it here), in the
inherent uneasiness in Plato's *Phaedrus*.

Although "The Oral Composition of Greek Drama" was first published
in 1980, some theory of postliterary tension was working its way into the
intelligentsia several decades before. To quote Havelock again, in his 1950
book *The Crucifixion of Intellectual Man*, the myth of the Fall in Genesis, as a
direct result of eating of the tree of knowledge, "gives poignant expression to
that conflict within the civilized consciousness of man, between his sense of
intellectual power and his distrust and fear of that power. . . . All the warmth
and the richness of man's nature demand that he live in the protection of
certain illusions in order to be secure, happy, and peaceful" (8). The "expected"
rather than the "invented." The further the artificial "memory" created by
textuality stretches back, and the more it can be built upon by an advancing
science, the more that security fades away. Man becomes dangerous and

also frightened. "Though our science may kill us, it will never allow us to retreat. Somehow we know that we would never burn enough books, nor eliminate enough intellectuals, to be able to return to the warm room" of blissful ignorance (9).

Within a decade of this assurance, two famous science fiction novels appeared dealing with the very attempt that Havelock had just pronounced futile: Ray Bradbury's *Fahrenheit 451* (1953) and Walter M. Miller's *A Canticle for Leibowitz* (1959). In *Fahrenheit 451* the protagonist, Guy Montag, is a "fireman"; that is, he burns forbidden books, and the houses that hide them, for a living. This is a busy job, considering the fact that just about all books are forbidden. There are a few rare exceptions, such as three-dimensional comic books, trade journals and, of course, rule books, those mainstays of any oppressive society. The rule book for the Firemen of America includes a brief history of the profession: "Established 1790, to burn English-influenced books in the Colonies. First Fireman: Benjamin Franklin" (30). According to the only available text, and to the voice of political authority, this is a glorious and time-honored profession, an idea that gives the firemen a sense of continuity and security . . . and, perhaps, allows Bradbury to make a comment on the fact that textual knowledge is power, even—or perhaps especially—false knowledge. Power becomes unbreachable if textual information is monolithic. According to the sinister but brilliant fire chief, Beatty, the main danger in books is that "none of those books agree with each other" (33, 54, 95). Very true, but a danger to whom? Peace of mind, he argues repeatedly. To one lawbreaker, kneeling despairingly amid her kerosene-soaked illegal books, Beatty cries, "You've been locked up here for years with a regular damned Tower of Babel. Snap out of it!" (33).

Inevitably, Montag becomes discontented with the status quo and curious about this nebulous "danger." Both his discontent and his curiosity are intensified when the woman mentioned above chooses to burn with her books rather than lose them. Beatty, seeing his distress when Montag feels "sick" and feigns illness, explains the real advent of the firemen in phrases that echo Havelock's concept of the loss of the "warm room" but takes it to its extreme limit:

> You always dread the unfamiliar. . . . We must all be alike. Not everyone born free and equal, as the Constitution says, but everyone made equal. Each man the image of every other; then all are happy, for there are no mountains to make them cower, to judge themselves against. (51)

On the literary side, he also echoes Plato on the "conceit of wisdom," and just how far that can be taken as a sort of leveling device:

Give the people contests they win by remembering the words to
more popular songs or the names of state capitals or how much
corn Iowa grew last year. Cram them full of noncombustible
data, chock them so damned full of 'facts' they feel stuffed, but
absolutely 'brilliant' with information. Then they'll feel they're
thinking, they'll get a *sense* of motion without moving. And
they'll be happy, because facts of that sort don't change. Don't give
them any slippery stuff like philosophy or sociology to tie things
up with. That way lies melancholy. (53–54)

These things are written, but they are not literature. The classicist may
be reminded here of the problems associated with Linear B, the proto-
Greek script found at Mycenae and Knossos. All of the inscriptions are "bald
counting-house dockets," (Palmer 13), "a text of the greatest interest" being
a tablet that "lists amounts of barley against various classes of craftsmen"
(Palmer 104). There is no literature *per se*, unless one were to use the standard
eighteenth-century definition of literature as "anything written." As a result,
it is difficult to get students interested in learning Linear B. There is simply
nothing interesting to read. The situation is described by Havelock as one
of preliteracy, in spite of the physical existence of written text: "whereas
historians who have touched upon literacy as a historical phenomenon have
commonly measured its progress in terms of the history of writing, the actual
conditions of literacy depend upon the history not of writing but of reading"
(*Literate Revolution* 56). One needs an audience. Get the audience to lose
interest, and you can do away with the literate civilization. In *Fahrenheit 451*
the reader has the feeling of moving backward in time to a preliterate society,
and the content of the society's "literature," although here it is for political
ends, strengthens this impression.

The last phrase of Beatty's pronouncement, "That way lies melancholy,"
with its literary overtones—very different from the plainer common speech
of his subordinates—is not unusual for Beatty. In keeping with the idea that
knowledge is power, Bradbury gives us several hints that the fire chief has had
frequent access to the forbidden texts and that this is either a cause or a result
of his being made chief (just which one is unclear). Like Kurt Vonnegut, Jr.'s
short story "Harrison Bergeron," set in another disturbing dystopia where
"everybody [is] finally equal" (7), some people are seen clearly to be more equal
than others and thus enabled to wield power over their fellows. In Vonnegut's
story, the ascendancy is physical: Diana Moon Glampers, the "Handicapper
General," is the only citizen who isn't decked out in distorting glasses,
distracting ear transmitters, and bags of birdshot to weaken her to the level of
society's lowest common denominator. In *Fahrenheit 451*, the ascendancy is
purely textual, but that is enough. Beatty's obnoxious confidence and habit of

quoting famous works strikes the reader immediately and leads to a question that Bradbury never answers: why is this highly literate person permitted to survive, let alone hold a position of high authority, in an aggressively oral society? Something is rotten in the whole system. Evidently someone higher up, Beatty's shadowy superior, feels that there is some inherent value in a well-read man, in spite of all the political rhetoric. This probability is directly opposed to Beatty's frequent deprecation of texts (a protection of his own monopoly?) and claim that the eventual ban of almost all books was not a political coup accomplished by a power-hungry elite at one fell swoop. Beatty's explanation, which we are never called upon to doubt, is that an outraged people seeking complete equality called for more and more censorship as texts became more widely available to interest groups that might be offended by them: "It didn't come from the Government down. There was no dictum, no declaration, no censorship, to start with, no! Technology, mass exploitation, and minority pressure carried the trick" (51). As Plato warned thousands of years earlier, well-read man had become an offensive "burden to his fellows."

Bradbury closes the novel, however, with an optimistic view: the text *will* prevail, and man will be the better for it. This is shown symbolically in the escape from the city by Montag and Faber, the only two literate men in the story besides Beatty—who, also symbolically, perishes in the same manner as the many books he has burned. The ignorant oral-culture citizens, radios tamped securely in their ears, remain in the city to be blown up by an enemy they could easily have escaped, if it weren't for the fact that their monolithic media preferred to keep them ignorant and happy. Having taken up with a group of itinerant professors, haltingly trying to remember the text of Ecclesiastes, Montag takes the first steps toward realizing the dream he had as he blindly fled the government's persecution: "Somewhere the saving and the putting away had to begin again and someone had to do the saving and keeping, one way or another, in books, in records, in people's heads, any way at all so long as it was safe, free from moths, silverfish, rust and dry-rot, and men with matches" (125).[1]

The idea that it is safe only when locked away in memory is almost a startling one in this book that so privileges the literary text; it seems as if the author has come full circle to an oral culture and the need to circumvent the shortcomings of Theuth's invention. Yet Bradbury makes it clear that they will write everything down as soon as possible and will try to reconstruct a fully literate society again. This should not take long, and is certainly desirable. The concept of text is a progressive thing, not a cyclical, and as long as any remnants remain there is always a base, however small, on which to build a better and wiser world.

A far more ambiguous view is present in *A Canticle for Leibowitz*. The loss of literacy here is not a gradual, internal thing, but a reactionary disruption. The survivors of nuclear war, emerging from their fallout shelters to face a devastated world and irreversible chromosome damage, realize that they have been shut out of Havelock's "warm room" for good. And they're angry. So, like Bradbury's people, they seek comfort and revenge by destroying all texts and all individuals connected with learning, escaping into a simple agrarian lifestyle very different from Bradbury's high-tech nightmare. One technician, Isaac Leibowitz, escapes, and hides among a group of Cistercian monks with a contraband collection of written material he has managed to save from the general purge. Eventually he is found out by the mob and martyred. But the texts, without him as interpreter, survive and are handed down from generation to generation. As Leibowitz takes on the trappings of sainthood, the texts become holy items—not for what they communicate, but for what they are, something he died to protect. The collection is eclectic: half a physics book here, three charred pages of mathematical equations there, an old book of fairy tales—anything the monks can get their hands on. For centuries these are passed down, their meaning becoming obscured, and this is where Miller's narrative begins.

The novel is set up in three sections, each set six hundred years apart from its predecessor. The first, postulating a civilization very like the European Dark Ages, deals with a novice named Brother Francis, who inadvertently discovers some new texts in an ancient fallout shelter six centuries after what the new scriptures refer to as the second, or Flame, Deluge (to distinguish it from Noah's flood). The characters in part 1 are innocent and superstitious, very like the civilization that spawned such works as Caedmon's hymn (which is often read as an allegory for the literate Christian world superseding the oral world of the pre-Christian, preliterate "heathens"). The choice of Cistercians is an appropriate one: not only does it associate the Abbey of the Blessed Leibowitz with Monte Cassino, that similar repository of learning and text, but "the organizational principles of movements like the Cistercians [in the middle ages] were clearly based on texts . . . Within the movement, texts were steps . . . by which the individual climbed toward a perfection thought to represent complete understanding and effortless communication with God" (Stock 90).

As Brian Stock points out, "one of the clearest signs that a group had passed the threshold of literacy was the lack of necessity for the organizing text to be spelt out, interpreted, or reiterated" (91). Brother Francis has not yet reached this level. In fact, Miller uses this lack of sophistication to humorous effect, showing how the monks have created a new oral mythos around the limited literature they have. When Francis discovers the fallout shelter (Maximum Occupancy: 15), he has enough literacy to read, but not to correctly interpret, the sign that identifies it:

were not the monsters of the world still called "children of the Fallout"? That the demon was capable of inflicting all the woes which descended upon Job was a recorded fact . . . [and] he had unwittingly broken into the abode (deserted he prayed) of not just one, but fifteen of the dreadful beings! (23)

The misinterpretation of the word "shelter" to mean a shelter *for*, rather than a shelter *from*, makes perfect grammatical sense. There is nothing wrong with Francis's reasoning, other than the fact that, as a semiotic critic would say, his sign system has broken down. When Francis runs into a similar problem over a memo reading, inexplicably, "Pound pastrami . . . can kraut, six bagels" (33), the monks' painstakingly reconstructed "literacy" turns out to be a world of signifiers with no corresponding signifieds to give them concrete meaning. Words have truly been reduced to phonemes, units of sound; the morphological substructure is incomplete and inappropriate.

The papers in the shelter bear the name of I. A. Leibowitz, and, as relics, focus attention on the literary Memorabilia of a past era. The Blessed Leibowitz is canonized and so, in a way, are the newfound papers: they are incorporated into the canon of the Memorabilia, to be copied by generations of monks who do not always understand what they are copying. Brother Francis, for instance, spends fifteen years producing a gorgeous illuminated and gold-leafed copy of the blueprint for a circuit board, and literally gives his life for it in a world where there has been no humanly generated electricity for six hundred years. The fact that he begins by questioning the possible sacrilege of copying the original backwards (black on white rather than white on black) and is later relieved of his anxiety when he finds a fragment explaining blueprints and realizes that since "the color scheme of the blueprints was an accidental feature of those ancient drawings . . . [a] glorified copy of the Leibowitz print could be made without incorporating the accidental feature" (89) is an additional semiotic joke on Miller's part. As they are copied, original documents are stored carefully away in lead-sealed, airtight casks, and faithful copies are made of the copies—with, of course, the occasional inevitable scribal mistake to provide a basis for future textual criticism.

Six hundred years after Brother Francis's discovery, the Abbey is still conducting itself along the same preliterate lines. Some advances in learning have been made, but not much of a practical nature. Although the naïveté is gone, it is still largely a case of learning solely for the disinterested sake of learning. There is a faint rumor of political conflict, but Hannegan, a local prince of Caesar-like ambition, is cheerfully illiterate and unlikely to show any interest in such an isolated area. This man has a literate cousin, however, who is very interested, indeed. Thon Taddeo receives permission to study the

Memorabilia, and his "rediscovery" and interpretation of these hidden works prompts a renaissance of learning.

This is not altogether a good thing. The first indications of a theme of antiliteracy are, perhaps, in the portrayal of the character of the Poet who has taken up residence in the Abbey. He is crude and ill-mannered, a trial to the monks' calm and ritualistic existence. In this way he is very like poetry itself—that is, lyric poetry of the sort that reached its apex of popularity in our own Victorian period. One may recall John Stuart Mill's distinction between (mere) eloquence and poetry: "eloquence is *heard*; poetry is overheard" (1038). The Poet is definitely of the overheard variety: "The Poet has always muttered," complains the prior (207). He is a highly literate character, as unpredictable and inventive—and despised—as Aristophanes's Euripides. Not too surprisingly, the only book that is mentioned in the entire novel as being read for pleasure is a book of "daring" verses that the abbot in part 3 pulls out, a book said to be written by "Saint Poet of the Miraculous Eyeball" (319), a reference to the Poet's glass eye. One might note that in part 3, when the world has become fully literate, the Poet is venerated as a saint, while in the semiliterate culture of part 2 he is regarded with mistrust and even dislike, for the most part. Marshall McLuhan identifies a similar mistrust in Pope's *Dunciad*, written at a period of increased circulation, and thus an increased reading audience, resulting in a stream of "self-indulgent" emotional poetry with no didactic purpose. He claims that "Book III [of the *Dunciad*] concerns the collective unconscious, the growing backwash from the tidal wave of self-expression. . . . Wit, the quick interplay among our senses and faculties, is thus steadily anaesthetized by the encroaching unconscious" (259). A similar annihilation occurs with the loss of the socially instructive function of poetry, the direct descendant of preliterate eras when Achilles and Agamemnon and Jesus Christ were presented as patterns for behavior.

In part 2 of *Canticle*, books are still either to be copied in the scriptorium or read aloud at communal meals (which, perhaps significantly, the Poet does not generally attend). Upon Thon Taddeo's arrival he is treated to a reading aloud of a scriptural account of the Flame Deluge, in highly ritualistic style: "But one of the magi was like unto Judas Iscariot, and his testimony was crafty, and having betrayed his brothers, he lied to all the people, advising them not to fear the demon Fallout" (198). The lesson contains a number of veiled warnings against the hubris of learning and the misuse of power, but Taddeo sweeps them all aside, disregarding everything but the archaic oralist language. He dismisses the warning as quaint, and heads for the library even as his retinue of soldiers begin sketching the Abbey's fortifications to report back to Hannegan its usefulness as a potential fortress—an action even more chilling when we consider it in the light of our own ill-conceived assault on Monte Cassino in 1944, a raid in which Miller took part and which was the partial genesis of *A Canticle for Leibowitz* (Ower 441). This secular influx, it is clear, bodes no good for the store of learning. A further note of foreboding is sounded when the Poet quits the monastery, leaving his glass eye with Taddeo: the abbot explains that as he was in the habit of removing the eye whenever he about to do something outrageous, the brothers and the Poet himself have come to refer to the eye as "the Poet's conscience." Taddeo replies, "So he thinks I need it more than he does" (237).

There are other parallels with our own literary history that come out in part 2, although Miller reverses the traditional role of the church vs. secular forces. Even as it is not writing, but reading, that defines a literate culture, in many ways it isn't so much writing, but *not*-writing, that is the political act. In a conference paper in 1981, Ong pointed out that "the totality of existence-saturated time is simply too much to manage" ("Oral Remembering" 13). The author has to pick and choose, simply by nature of his medium. Ong illustrates this with a quotation from the book of John: "There are still many other things that Jesus did, yet if they were written about in detail, I doubt there would be room enough in the entire world to hold the books to record them" (21:25). In this case, the choice is clear: "the author picks from Jesus's life what is particularly relevant to human beings' salvation" ("Oral Remembering" 13). The issue of what gets preserved is a similar one. Jeff Opland reminds us in his book on *Anglo Saxon Oral Poetry* that much of what is reported about poetry, and what poetry we have, is inextricably tied up with church politics and what the Catholic Church deemed worthy of preservation. Basically, it comes down to a situation of who has the vellum.

The extreme of this is, of course, Orwell's *1984*, but it is also an aspect of preliteracy. The Sapir-Whorf hypothesis—the idea that our language shapes our perceptions of reality—is most easily observed in preliterate cultures. Their values, their thought, and even their vocabulary is much more homogeneous: "Sapir-Whorfian notions of cultural relativity in distinctions encoded within differing languages apply more obviously to cultures which have remained primarily oral ... since oral cultures, lacking dictionaries, delete from the lexicon as well as create distinctions within it according to the criterion of current social usefulness" (Durant 337).

Miller's monks are aware of this in a subconscious sort of way, and attempt to maintain a homogeneity of cherishing everything equally. To them, all texts are holy, and they continue to treasure their illuminated grocery lists long after they have grown sophisticated enough to realize that these texts are likely to be of doubtful utility. Text is above utility or politics and has entered the realm of the sacred, taking on almost the mystic quality of runes, or the writing on a well-known Greek cup dating back to preliterate days: "Whoso drinks this drinking cup straight-way him / Desire shall seize of fair-crowned Aphrodite" (Havelock, *Literate Revolution* 195). Writing itself has the power, rather than the person who exploits it. Taddeo never realizes this. Even as he travels toward the Abbey he explains to the nomad tribes which are providing him with an escort that he is seeking "*incantations* of great power" (174; italics are Miller's) that will be of tactical use for him.

By not giving privilege to any particular genre or subject, the monks have effectively depoliticized the medium, a situation that comes to an abrupt end when Taddeo comes along to make distinctions between what is useful and what is not. Thus Taddeo's rediscovery of the Memorabilia is not just a renaissance of science but also a revolution in the role of text as communication rather than text as object. The change in role is not accomplished without some trepidation on the part of the more conservative monks, in particular the librarian: "To the custodian of the Memorabilia, each unsealing represented another decrease in the probable lifetime of the contents of the cask, and he made no attempt to conceal his disapproval of the entire proceeding. To Brother Librarian, whose task in life was the preservation of books, the principal reason for the existence of books was that they might be preserved perpetually" (209–10).

The librarian is the extreme case, but even the abbot is concerned about such an abrupt and complete dissemination of texts, as he confides to Taddeo in one of the most important passages in the book:

> You promise to begin restoring Man's control over Nature. But who will govern the use of the power to control natural forces? Who will use it? To what end? Such decisions can still be made. But if you and your group don't make them now, others will soon make them for you. Mankind will profit, you say. By whose sufferance? The sufferance of a prince who signs his letters X? (238)

This is the turning point. As Alan Durant remarks, "literacy leads to a diversification of, and contradictions within, previously homogeneous 'oral' cultures, as readers are differentially influenced by earlier stages of the cultural record, interpret them differently, and use them to support divergent versions of aspiration and intent"(337). This is what Beatty was warning of in *Fahrenheit 451*, and now it is what Thon Taddeo opens up. When the abbot pleads with him to slow down his investigations and keep destructive information out of Hannegan's hands, Taddeo characteristically misinterprets him and believes that he is forcing religion down his throat. "'Would you have me work for the Church?'The scorn in his voice was unmistakable" (239).

As a result of Taddeo's reintroduction of the Memorabilia to the general public, six centuries later "there were spaceships again" (258) and electric lights and newspapers and all manner of technological marvels. When we first meet the third and final abbot he is being held at bay by an "Abominable Autoscribe,"a machine that converts oral text to written (and, if necessary, into a foreign language, to boot). The fact that it doesn't work is indicative of the difficulties of all writing: having lost the ability to communicate orally—the abbot is trying to write a letter to a cardinal who doesn't speak his language—he finds himself at the mercy of an imperfect technology. Yet he admits that "I don't trust my own Anglo-Latin, and if I did, *he'd* probably not trust his" (266). As Socrates's King of Egypt predicted, the medium that was meant to increase memory has actually decreased it, with potentially disastrous results: the aborted letter was a request for orders concerning Operation Peregrinatur, a plan to evacuate selected members of the Order to the off-world colonies on Alpha Centauri, since it has become obvious that history has repeated itself and mankind is once again manufacturing nuclear weapons.

Inevitably, war does come and the Operation is put into effect. Having lost their function as guardians of the Memorabilia, the monks spend all of part 3 desperately trying to escape its effects. As "the visage of Lucifer mushroom[s] into hideousness above the cloudbank, rising slowly like some titan climbing to its feet after ages of imprisonment in the Earth" (355), the starship lifts into the sky with a cargo of twenty-seven monks, six nuns, twenty children ... and the Memorabilia, preserved *in toto* on microfilm. "It was no curse, this knowledge, unless perverted by Man, as fire had been, this night" (303). But of course it will be, eventually. Text, with the seeds of destruction encoded within it, follows Man like a recurring damnation. Man, the textual animal, will Deconstruct the universe.

Both *A Canticle for Liebowitz* and *Fahrenheit 451* end with a nuclear apocalypse and a new literacy springing from the ashes. Bradbury's positive, progressive view of literary history contrasts sharply with Miller's negative, cyclical view, just as Bradbury's depiction of a predominately oral culture as mind-numbing contrasts with Miller's depiction of orality as the preserver of ritual and collective human values. One might conclude this paper with the Unanswerable Question so popular with medieval bards at the ends of their stories: "Which point of view is the correct one?" And, as it has always been, the correct answer is "both."

NOTE

1. This, of course, is a Biblical echo: "lay up for yourselves treasures in heaven, where neither moth nor rust doth corrupt, and where thieves do not break through nor steal" (Matthew 6:20).

WORKS CITED

Bradbury, Ray. *Fahrenheit 451*. New York: Ballantine, 1979.

Derrida, Jacques. *Dissemination*. Trans. Barbara Johnson. Chicago: U of Chicago P, 1981.

Durant, Alan. "The Concept of Secondary Orality: Observations about Speech and Text in Modern Communications Media." *Dalhousie Review* 64 (Summer 1984): 332–53.

Havelock, Eric A. *The Literate Revolution in Greece and Its Cultural Consequences*. Princeton, NJ: Princeton UP, 1982.

———. *The Crucifixion of Intellectual Man*. Boston: Beacon Press, 1951.

McLuhan, Marshall. *The Gutenberg Galaxy*. Toronto: U of Toronto P, 1962.

Mill, John Stuart. "What is Poetry?" *Norton Anthology of English Literature*. Vol. 2. Ed. M. H. Abrams et al. New York: Norton, 1986.

Miller, Walter M., Jr. *A Canticle for Leibowitz*. London: Black Swan, 1984.

Ong, Walter S. *Orality and Literacy: The Technologizing of the Word*. New York: Methuen, 1982.

———. "Oral Remembering and Narrative Structures." *Analyzing Discourse: Text and Talk. Georgetown University Round Table on Languages and Linguistics 1981*. Ed. Deborah Tannen. Washington, DC: Georgetown UP, 1982. 12–24.

Opland, Jeff. *Anglo Saxon Oral Poetry: A Study of the Traditions*. New Haven, CT: Yale UP, 1980.

Ower, John B. "Walter M. Miller, Jr." in *Science Fiction Writers: Critical Studies of the Major Authors from the Early Nineteenth Century to the Present Day*. Ed. E. F. Bleiler. New York: Scribner, 1982. 441–48.

Palmer, Leonard R. *Myceneans and Minoans: Aegean Prehistory in the Light of the Linear B Tablets*. New York: Knopf, 1962.

Plato, *Phaedrus*. Trans. R. Hackforth. *Plato: Collected Dialogues*. Ed. Edith Hamilton and Huntington Cairns. Princeton, NJ: Princeton UP, 1961.

Stock, Brian. *The Implications of Literacy*. Princeton, NJ: Princeton UP, 1983.

Vonnegut, Kurt, Jr. "Harrison Bergeron." *Welcome to the Monkey House*. New York: Dell, 1970. 7–13.

DIANE S. WOOD

Bradbury and Atwood:
Exile as Rational Decision

Ray Bradbury's *Fahrenheit 451* and Margaret Atwood's *The Handmaid's Tale* depict the rational decision to go into exile, to leave one's native land, that is, the pre-exile condition. These novels present horrifying views of the near future where societal pressures enforce rigid limitations on individual freedom. Their alienated characters find their circumstances repugnant. Justice and freedom are denied them, along with the possibility for enriching their lives through intellectual pursuits. These speculative novels like Orwell's *1984* are dystopian in nature, showing how precarious are today's constitutional rights and how necessary it is to preserve these liberties for future generations. They depict ordinary people, caught in circumstances that they cannot control, people who resist oppression at the risk of their lives and who choose exile because it *has* to be better than their present, unbearable circumstances. Voluntary exile necessitates a journey into the unknown as an alternative to the certain repression of the present.

Both novels offer a bleak possible future for the United States. Bradbury, writing in the McCarthy era of the 1950s, envisions a time when people choose to sit by the hour watching television programs and where owning books is a crime. Atwood, in the 1980s, foresees a time when, in the wake of changes begun during the Reagan Administration, women are denied even the most basic rights of working and owning property.[1] Both novels thus

From *The Literature of Emigration and Exile*, edited by James Whitlark and Wendell Aycock, pp. 131–142. © 1992 by Texas Tech University Press.

present "political" stances in the widest sense of the word. In her address on Amnesty International, Atwood defines the word "politics" and how it comes to be incorporated into a writer's work:

> By 'politics' I do not mean how you voted in the last election, although that is included. I mean who is entitled to do what to whom, with impunity; who profits by it; and who therefore eats what. Such material enters a writer's work not because the writer is or is not consciously political but because a writer is an observer, a witness, and such observations are the air he breathes. They are the air all of us breathe; the only difference is that the author looks, and then writes down what he sees. What he sees will depend on how closely he looks and at what, but look he must. (1982, 394)

To Atwood being "political" is part of the moral stance of the writer as truth teller. In his 1966 Introduction to *Fahrenheit 451*, Bradbury expresses moral outrage concerning bookburning: "when Hitler burned a book I felt it as keenly, please forgive me, as his killing a human, for in the long sum of history they are one and the same flesh. Mind or body, put to the oven, is a sinful practice...."[2] He sees the necessity to guard constantly against such practices:

> For while Senator McCarthy has long been dead, the Red Guard in China comes alive and idols are smashed, and books, all over again, are thrown into the furnace. So it will go, one generation printing, another generation burning, yet another remembering what is good to remember so as to print again. (14)

Atwood stresses the qualities of authors which make them a danger to oppressive governments: "The writer, unless he is a mere word processor, retains three attributes that power-mad regimes cannot tolerate: a human imagination, in the many forms it may take; the power to communicate; and hope." (1982, 397)

The novels by Bradbury and Atwood examine the personal response of an individual who is in conflict with the majority in his society and whose occupation is abhorrent to him. *Fahrenheit 451* centers upon the personal crisis of Montag, a young fireman whose job consists of burning books. He finds his life increasingly meaningless and eventually comes to reject the too-simple, clichéd values of his milieu. He experiences loneliness in a society where people are constantly entertained without time given to reflexion and personal development, activities often associated with the reading process.

The more complicated nuances of the world of books are available to him only when he leaves his reductionistic society. Atwood's novel recounts the story of a protagonist caught up in the rapid transition of her society. Dehumanized, stripped of her personal name and individual identity, and referred to only by the name of the man to whose household she is assigned, Offred (or Of-Fred), a handmaid, experiences firsthand an upheaval in the social order ending in limited personal freedom.[3] The new oligarchy uses Old Testament injunctions to justify extreme repression. Like the shock troops to which they are compared (144), handmaids are in the *avant garde* of the social reform and they undergo brutal re-education at the Rachel & Leah Re-Education Centers, after which, like soldiers, they are "posted" to a commander's household. Even more than Montag, Offred's life is determined by her social role. As a fertile woman in a nearly sterile society, her function is to produce viable offspring and her entire life is regulated by her reproductive duties.[4] She describes herself and her fellow handmaids as "two-legged wombs, that's all: sacred vessels, ambulatory chalices" (1985, 176). There is nothing erotic about the handmaids, their mission is strictly biological: "We are for breeding purposes: we aren't concubines, geisha girls, courtesans" (176). Whereas Montag has to seek out an understanding of how his society developed, Offred lives through the transitional period and is thus acutely aware of the stages on the way to losing individual freedom. From the beginning of the narrative, she is literally a prisoner, watched at all times and even tattooed with a number: "Four digits and an eye, a passport in reverse. It's supposed to guarantee that I will never be able to fade, finally, into another landscape. I am too important, too scarce, for that. I am a national resource" (84–5).

In both novels the population is strictly regulated and the conduct of individuals is highly regimented. Indeed, in these repressive circumstances, it is not surprising that the protagonists would wish to flee, especially since, by the end of the novels, they have broken laws which would bring the death penalty if they were apprehended. "Mechanical Hounds" use scent to hunt down lawbreakers in Bradbury's fiction.[5] The hounds tear apart their prey. Montag narrowly escapes this fate but the police do not admit being outwitted. They stage his death for the benefit of the huge television audience which follows the developing story of his evasion.[6] The authorities murder an innocent derelict in Montag's place, so as not to disappoint the viewers and appear ineffectual. The authorities are motivated by the desire to maintain power at any cost and blatantly violate human rights.

Discipline is less mechanized in *The Handmaid's Tale* but no less ruthless. Cadres of brutal "Aunts," "Angels," "Guardians," and "Eyes" enforce order in Atwood's imaginary Gilead. Cattleprods punish uncooperative handmaids in the rehabilitation center. For particularly bad infractions, the handmaids' hands and feet are tortured: "They used steel cables, frayed at the ends. After that the hands. They didn't care what they did to your feet or your hands, even if it was permanent. Remember, said Aunt Lydia. For our purposes your feet and your hands are not essential" (118).[7] Other punishments are even more severe. A woman caught reading three times merits a hand cut off. Handmaids are executed for being unchaste, attempting to kill a commander, or trying to escape. Wives die for adultery or for attempting to kill a handmaid. As in the Middle Ages, cadavers of tortured prisoners are displayed on the town wall to encourage conformity to rules.[8] Offred describes her reaction to the cadavers hanging there:

> It's the bags over the heads that are the worst, worse than the faces themselves would be. It makes the men like dolls on which the faces have not yet been painted; like scarecrows, which in away is what they are, since they are meant to scare. Or as if their heads are sacks, stuffed with some undifferentiated material, like flour or dough. It's the obvious heaviness of the heads, their vacancy, the way gravity pulls them down and there's no life anymore to hold them up. The heads are zeros. (43)

Execution is a public event, called a "Salvaging."[9] The local women are assembled to witness the execution by hanging of two handmaids and a wife. The authorities decide to depart from past procedure and not read the crimes of the condemned in order to prevent a rash of similar crimes. Offred comments on the unpopularity of this decision: "The crimes of others are a secret language among us. Through them we show ourselves what we might be capable of, after all" (354). The assembled women are required to assent to the punishment even though they do not know the nature of the crime. As part of the audience, Offred makes the ceremonial gesture of compliance with the execution: "I . . . then placed my hand on my heart to show my unity with the Salvagers and my consent, and my complicity in the death of this woman" (355).

An even more frightening public ceremony is that of "Particicution," where handmaids act as executioners of an accused rapist. Death is the punishment set in Deuteronomy 22:23–29. Offred paints the scene in terms of bloodlust: "The air is bright with adrenaline, we are permitted anything and this is freedom" (359). The women literally tear the accused apart with their bare hands. These brutal ceremonies serve to release violent emotion in a socially approved setting, since its normal expression is otherwise denied.

The major task of both Bradbury and Atwood is to portray convincingly in their futuristic novels how the abridgement of freedom evolved in the United States. As such, the novels are strong political statements warning of the consequences of what seem dangerous trends to the authors. One has only to look at the statistics for television watching, witness the decline of interest in reading among our students, and read current reports about ecological damage to verify the gravity of the dangers this country faces at the present time. In the world of *Fahrenheit 451* people have given up thinking for mindless pursuits. No revolution or *coup d'etat* brings about the loss of freedom. Rather, individual laziness precipitates a gradual erosion. This evolution takes place long before the birth of Montag, who grows up in a society where books are proscribed. His superior, a fireman, explains the trend of increasing simplification as the result of the influence of the mass media: "Things began to have *mass*. . . . And because they had mass, they became simpler. . . . Once, books appealed to a few people, here, there, everywhere. They could afford to be different. The world was roomy. But then the world got full of eyes and elbows and mouths (61). In a vast generalization which is itself a simplification, he tells how the modern era brought a movement to speed up and condense everything:

> Then, in the twentieth century, speed up your camera. Books cut shorter. Condensations. Digests. Tabloids. Everything boils down to the gag, the snap ending. . . . Classics cut to fit fifteen-minute radio shows, then cut again to fill a two-minute book column, winding up at last as a ten- or twelve-line dictionary resume. . . . Do you see? Out of the nursery into the college and back to the nursery; there's your intellectual pattern for the past five centuries or more (61)

The rich value of books is thus denied when they are reduced to brief summaries. Happiness to this fireman comes from eliminating all dissension, especially that caused by books: "'Colored people don't like Little Black Sambo. Burn it. White people don't feel good about Uncle Tom's Cabin. Burn it. Someone's written a book on tobacco and cancer of the lungs? The cigarette people are weeping? Burn the book. Serenity, Montag. Peace, Montag. Take your fight outside. Better yet, into the incinerator'" (65–6). Yet this society does not produce happiness. Montag is perpetually lonely and his wife attempts suicide.

Whereas Atwood's society ceremonializes violence, in Bradbury's book the society eliminates all cause for unhappiness and sweeps unpleasantness away, including those which are an integral part of the human condition: "'Funerals are unhappy and pagan? Eliminate them, too. Five minutes after a person is dead he's on his way to the Big Flue, the Incinerators serviced by helicopters all over the country. Ten minutes after death a man's a speck of black dust. Let's not quibble over individuals with memoriams. Forget them. Burn all, burn everything. Fire is bright and fire is clean'" (66). Television concerns itself with the ephemeral present and thus follows the trend toward forgetting the past.[10] Books by their very essence preserve and memorialize those who have lived before. Bradbury would probably agree with Atwood's comments that all repressive governments eliminate authors because they are so dangerous.[11] The fireman views fire as a means of purging and cleansing emotions in his society. Political dissension is eliminated by giving only one side of the argument (66). War is not even talked about (66). People are reduced to thinking about simple facts, meaningless data: "Cram them full of noncombustible data, chock them so full of 'facts' they feel stuffed, but absolutely 'brilliant' with information. Then they'll feel they're thinking, they'll get a *sense* of motion without moving. And they'll be happy, because facts of that sort don't change. Don't give them any slippery stuff like philosophy or sociology to tie things up with. That way lies melancholy" (56). Through simplifying and reducing ideas, he feels that the firemen produce happiness for the society: "'we're the Happiness Boys, the Dixie Duo, you and I and the others. We stand against the small tide of those who want to make everyone unhappy with conflicting theory and thought. We have our fingers in the dike. Hold steady. Don't let the torrent of melancholy and drear philosophy drown our world'" (67).

Balancing this reductionist apology are the views of another character in the novel, a retired English professor who "had been thrown out upon the world forty years ago when the last liberal arts college shut for lack of students and patronage" (76). He traces the lack of reading to apathy: "Remember, the firemen are rarely necessary. The public itself stopped reading of its own accord. Your firemen provide a circus now and then at which buildings are set off and crowds gather for the pretty blaze, but it's a small sideshow indeed, and hardly necessary to keep things in line. So few want to be rebels anymore. And out of those few, most, like myself, scare easily" (87). The professor's personal experience bears witness to the gradual nature of the transition from a reading to a non-reading culture. One day, there are simply no more students:

> That was a year I came to class at the start of the new semester and found only one student to sign up for Drama from Aeschylus to O'Neill. You see? How like a beautiful statue of ice it was, melting in the sun. I remember the newspapers dying like huge moths. No one wanted them back. No one missed them. And then the Government, seeing low advantageous it was to have people reading only about passionate lips and the fist in the stomach, circled the situation with your fire-eaters. (88)[12]

Whereas in *Fahrenheit 451* the government acted opportunistically, taking advantage of the lack of passionate readers to outlaw books, the government in *The Handmaid's Tale* actively shapes lifestyles through public policy. Atwood's protagonist recalls the governmental action that declares women may no longer own property and hold jobs (227–31). Offred is fired, along with every other woman in the country. Her money can be transferred to her husband, but she no longer may control the funds accessed by her plastic card. The government deprives women of the right to work and to own property simultaneously, to prevent a mass exodus (231}. These freedoms were not the first to be lost, however. Offred explains the progressive loss of the women's constitutional rights, perpetrated by an ominous invisible group she identifies as "they":

> It was after the catastrophe, when *they* shot the president and machine-gunned the Congress and the army declared a state of emergency. *They* blamed it on the Islamic fanatics, at the time. . . . That was when *they* suspended the Constitution. *They* said it would be temporary. There wasn't even any rioting in the streets. People stayed home at night, watching television, looking for some direction. There wasn't even an enemy you could put your finger on. (225, emphasis mine)

Still the transition is gradual and required the complicity of the populace: "We lived, as usual, by ignoring. Ignoring isn't the same as ignorance, you have to work at it. Nothing changes instantaneously: in a gradually heating bathtub you'd be boiled to death before you knew it" (74).[13] The protagonist finally decides that the conditions of the military state are untenable and unsuccessfully tries to escape to freedom with her husband and child, only to find that it is too late. When captured, she is separated from her family whom she never sees again, and is forced to take her place as a handmaid.

In both novels books represent important artifacts of the past and the act of reading becomes a heroic gesture. This is not surprising since both authors are avid readers and have described the importance of books in their lives. In fact, *Fahrenheit 451* was written in the UCLA library (15).[14] One of the most crucial passages in the novel shows a woman willing to die for her books. Montag is stunned when she sets fire to her library and immolates herself along with her precious volumes.[15] This experience causes Montag to question what there is in books that is worth dying for and ultimately leads to his becoming a preserver of books instead of a destroyer.[16] Allusions to being denied the right to read occur throughout *The Handmaid's Tale*. As a handmaid, Offred is forbidden to read, a hardship for a person whose former job was in a library. The only words she sees are "faith" on the petit point cushion in her room and "*Nolite te bastardes carborundorum*" (Don't let the bastards get you down) which is scratched in tiny letters near the floor of her cupboard. During the course of the novel Offred recalls reading and having access to books and regrets her former blasé attitude toward them. Because they are now denied to her, they become very precious whereas once books were commonplace and taken for granted. In the middle of the novel her Commander (the Fred of Offred) invites her to forbidden soirees in his private study. He permits her to read old women's magazines. Offred philosophically reflects on the promise that the old magazines once held:

> What was in them was promise. They dealt in transformations; they suggested an endless series of possibilities, extending like the reflections in two mirrors set facing one another, stretching on, replica after replica, to the vanishing point. They suggested one adventure after another, one wardrobe after another, one improvement after another, one man after another. They suggested rejuvenation, pain overcome and transcended, endless love. The real promise in them was immortality. (201)

The Commander not only lets Offred read magazines but plays scrabble with her. This is the ultimate in forbidden games in a society where women are not allowed to read: "Now it's dangerous. Now it's indecent. Now it's something he can't do with his Wife. Now it's desirable. Now he's compromised himself. It's as if he's offered me drugs" (179).

When the Commander allows Offred to read magazines, the experience is equated to the orgiastic pleasures of eating or of sex: "On these occasions I read quickly, voraciously, almost skimming, trying to get as much into my head as possible before the next long starvation. If it were eating it would be the gluttony of the famished; if it were sex it would be a swift furtive stand-up in an alley somewhere" (239, and see 1988, 110). The Commander, who watches the illicit reading, is described as a sort of pervert: "While I read, the Commander sits and watches me doing it, without speaking but also without taking his eyes off me. This watching is a curiously sexual act, and I feel undressed while he does it. I wish he would turn his back, stroll around the room, read something himself. Then perhaps I could relax more, take my time. As it is, this illicit reading of mine seems a kind of performance" (239).

These magazines somehow escaped the government's attention, although house-to-house searches and bonfires were conducted on the orders of the oligarchy in order to remove all reading material from women (202). The government of Gilead denied women access to the printed word as a means of controlling them.[17] Only the vicious Aunts are allowed to read and write as a part of their role in re-educating the handmaids (166), The effect of this is to silence the women, or as Atwood has said elsewhere: "The aim of all suppression is to silence *the voice*, abolish the word, so that the only voices and words left are those of the ones in power" (see 1982, 350).

In her essays Atwood speaks out against suppression of reading and writing, abhorring fascism on anyone's part.[18] This view is paralleled in the novel where Offred remembers as a young girl attending a magazine burning with her mother, who is recalled as a quintessential feminist demonstrator of the 1970s. As the pornographic material burns the image evoked is particularly poetic: "I threw the magazine into the flames. It rifled open in the wind of its burning; big flakes of paper came loose, sailed into the air, still on fire, parts of women's bodies, turning to black ash, in the air, before my eyes" (51). Offred's views toward women's rights are much less activist in nature than her mother's. The mother/daughter relationship is fraught with tension and their opposing viewpoints brings into question some of the tactics of the women's movement including the bookburning. After attending a "Birthing," a particularly grotesque woman's ritual in Gilead, Offred ironically comments: "Mother, I think. Wherever you may be. Can you hear me? You wanted a women's culture. Well now there is one. It isn't what you meant, but it exists. Be thankful for small mercies" (164). Her feminist mother probably dies a victim of the new regime, but when Gilead comes into being, there is no triumph on the part of the rightwing opponents to the woman's movement like the Commander's Wife Serena Joy. These women also find no happiness in the new society.

Despite the fact that the social order is founded on biblical references, women are not allowed to read the Bible: "The Bible is kept locked up, the way people once kept tea locked up, so the servants wouldn't steal it. It is an incendiary device: who knows what we'd make of it, if we ever got our hands on it? We can be read to from it, by him [the commander], but we cannot read" (112). Even the familiar reading passages read by the commander hold their attraction for those hungering for the written word: "He's like a man toying with a steak, behind a restaurant window, pretending not to see the eyes watching him from hungry darkness not three feet from his elbow. We lean towards him a little, iron flings to his magnet. He has something we don't have, he has the word. How we squandered it, once" (114). Tapes of biblical readings are an integral part of the re-education in the Rachel and Leah Centers. The quotations, however, have been changed to further the goals of the oligarchy. Offred notices transformations in the Beatitudes: "*Blessed be the poor in spirit, for theirs is the kingdom of heaven. Blessed are the merciful. Blessed be the meek. Blessed are the silent.* I knew they made that up, I knew it was wrong, and they left things out, too, but there was no way of checking. *Blessed be those that mourn, for they shall be comforted.* Nobody said when" (115). Her ironic comments underscore her frustration with the prohibition against reading and her resistance to indoctrination.

Just as the Beatitudes are rewritten, Marx's comments about the distribution of property are attributed to the Bible in order to justify the distribution of the precious and scarce handmaids in Gilead: "Not every Commander has a Handmaid: some of their Wives have children. *From each*, says the slogan, *according to her ability; to each according to his needs*. We recited that, three times, after dessert. It was from the Bible, or so they said. St. Paul again, in Acts" (151).

The author's ironic use of religious terms becomes comic when she creates the franchise "Soul Scrolls" where prayers are continually spewed out on printout machines called "Holy Rollers" and paid for by pious citizens. Like the flavors in an ice cream store, there are five different prayers: "for health, wealth, a death, a birth, a sin" (216). The state religion distortedly caricatures fundamentalist beliefs, including having a former television gospel singer as the Commander's Wife.

Each novel ends with the protagonist's escape and the beginning of his exile from repression. There is some ambiguity, however, since the alternative order is not elaborated on. Montag watches his city being destroyed by a nuclear explosion. He joins a group of vagabonds who memorize the books with which they have escaped. No attempt is made to follow his further development in these difficult circumstances or to predict the course the future holds for society or the survivors.[19] "The implication is clear, however, that intellectual freedom is worth the inconvenience of life outside the modern city. Because he left, Montag survives the death of the mindless masses who stayed behind. Offred's fate is even more ambiguous. In the last lines of her tale she describes her feelings as she steps into the Black Maria which has come for her: "Whether this is my end or a new beginning I have no way of knowing: I have given myself over into the hands of strangers, because it can't be helped. And so I step up, into the darkness within; or else the light" (378). The postscript "Historical Notes on *The Handmaid's Tale*" provides information that the heroine survives to record her story on cassette tapes.[20] She is rescued by the Mayday organization of the Underground Femaleroad (381–2). Her ultimate fate is unknown to the scholars of 2195 who, in an academic conference, comment on the handmaid's story as a historical document from the past.[21]

The appeal of these two highly acclaimed novels stems from the main characters' difficult situation in a repressive future United States. The plausible explanations given by both Bradbury and Atwood for the ghastly turn taken by American society in the futures they portray serves as a vivid reminder that freedom must be vigilantly guarded in order to be maintained. Apathy and fear create unlivable societies from which only a few courageous souls dare escape. "Ordinary" says one of the cruel Aunts of *The Handmaid's Tale* "is what you are used to" (45). The main characters never are able to accept the "ordinariness" of the repression which surrounds them. They are among the few who are willing to risk the difficult path of exile.

Notes

1. Arthur A. Davidson in "Future Tense: Making History" (in 1988, 113) points out how "the appalling future [is] already implicit in the contemporary world." It is the very plausibility of these futures that make them so terrifying.

2. Not all critics see the political nature of this novel. For Wayne L. Johnson, "The book is about as far as Bradbury has come in the direction of using science fiction for social criticism" (see 1980, 85). He considers "Montag's spiritual development" to be the main focus of the novel (87).

3. Roberta Rubenstein points out that Offred's name always is akin to "offered" and views the name as encoding "her indentured sexuality." See her "Nature and Nurture in Dystopia" in 1988, 103.

4. Rubenstein relates the female anxieties in the novel to "female ambivalence about childbearing in patriarchy" (102).

5. Donald Watt comments on the symbolic nature of the hounds who lurk in the dark and then relentlessly pursue and execute "those who seek to shed some light on their age" in his "Burning Bright: *Fahrenheit 451* as Symbolic Dystopia," (1980, 201).

6. Watt considers the audience to be more menacing than the Mechanical Hound (212). Peter Sisario terms the television entertainment "tapioca-bland" (in 1970, 201).

7. Rubenstein discusses how bodies are objectified and reduced to their parts, a critique begun in Atwood's *Bodily Harm* (1982, 103–5). She also draws an interesting parallel with the binding of female feet among the Chinese.

8. The novel thereby suggests that such tactics are a part of the modern world, a notion Atwood has underscored in her essays "Witches" (332–3) and "Amnesty International" (396) in *Second Words*.

9. Rubenstein demonstrates the ironic resonances of "salvaging" with "*salvage, salvation,* and *savaging*" (104).

10. See Marvin D. Mengeling's "The Machineries of Joy and Despair" (in 1980, 95). David Mogen sees this "reductionist, materialist image of human nature and human culture reinforced through mass entertainment media" as a peculiarity of American culture (in 1986, 107).

11. Because of her view of the role of the author, Atwood has strong words to say about torture:

> One of the few remedies for it is free human speech, which is why writers are always among the first to be lined up against the wall by any totalitarian regime, left or right. How many poets are there in El Salvador? The answer is none. They have all been shot or exiled. The true distinction in the world today is not between the so-called left and the so-called right. It's between the governments that do such things as a matter of policy, or that wink at them when they are done, and those that do not. ("Witches" in 1982, 332)

12. Atwood addresses the problem of apathetic readership in her essay "An End to Audience?" (in 1982). She posits the concept "free reading" as a corollary to free speech (354).

13. Davidson sees the protagonist as an essentially passive character who goes along with the changes until the situation becomes untenable (116). She complies rather than instigates action.

14. Willis C. McNelly speaks of Bradbury's "lifelong love affair with books," equating Montag with the author in "I. Ray Bradbury—Past, Present, and Future" (in 1980, 19).

15. Watt sees this woman demonstrating for Montag "the possibility of defiance and the power of books" (198). See also 201–2.

16. Watt sees the group outside the city as the preserver of human culture (210). Mengeling's terms Montag's metamorphosis as a change "from book-burner to living-book" (86).

17. Atwood's praise of Tillie Olsen's *Silences* in *Second Words* bears witness to her concern about silencing women (313–5). Barbara Hill Rigney finds that the principal subject of this novel is "the suppression of language, especially language used by women" (in 1987, 131).

18. Helen N. Buss speaks to the question of the bookburning: "The caution here is that if feminists seek fascist solutions they are ultimately condoning fascism" in her forthcoming article "Maternity and Narrative Strategies in the Novels of Margaret Atwood." Rigney concurs with Buss's assessment of Atwood's criticism of the tactics of certain feminists: "In *The Handmaid's Tale*, as in the actual and current situation, some feminist groups exercise the same faulty judgment, thereby forfeiting their own freedom along with that of both the writers and the reading audience" (134).

19. Johnson points out the uncertainty of the novel's ending both for Montag and for the future of the society (88).

20. Rubenstein makes the pertinent comment that Offred's story is an act of self-generation which opposes the procreation duties required of a handmaid (105).

21. Davidson's article offers insight into Atwood's presentation of the academic community in the epilogue. He notes the pessimism implicit in this ending (120). Rubenstein, on the other hand, sees its comic aspects (111–2).

Works Cited

Atwood, Margaret. *Bodily Harm*. Toronto: McClelland and Stewart, 1977.

———. *The Handmaid's Tale*. New York: Fawcett Crest, 1985.

———. *Second Words, Selected Critical Prose*. Toronto: Anansi, 1982.

Bradbury, Ray. *Fahrenheit 451*. New York: Simon and Schuster, 1967.

Buss, Helen N. "Maternity and Narrative Strategies in the Novels of Margaret Atwood," *Atlantis* 15 (1): [forthcoming].

Greenberg, Martin Harry and Joseph D. Olander. *Ray Bradbury*. New York: Taplinger, 1980.

Johnson, Wayne L. *Ray Bradbury*. New York: Frederick Ungar, 1980.

Mogen, David. *Ray Bradbury*. Boston, Twayne, 1986.

Olsen, Tillie. *Silences*. New York: Laurif Seymour Lawrence, 1983.

Peter Sisario. "A Study of Allusions in Bradbury's *Fahrenheit 451*," *English Journal* 59 (1970): 201.

Rigney, Barbara Hill. *Margaret Atwood*. Totowa, NJ: Barnes & Nobel, 1987.

VanSpanckeren, Kathryn and Jan Garden Castro. Eds. *Margaret Atwood, Vision and Forms*. Carbondale and Edwardsville: S. Illinois University Press, 1988.

RAY BRADBURY

Burning Bright

February 14, 1993

Five short jumps and then a huge leap.

Five ladyfinger firecrackers and then an explosion.

That just about describes the genesis of *Fahrenheit 451*.

Five short stories, written over a period of two or three years, caused me to invest nine dollars and fifty cents in dimes to rent a pay typewriter in a basement library typing room and finish the short novel in just nine days.

How so?

The small jumps, the small firecrackers, first:

In a brief story, "Bonfire," which never sold to any magazine, I imagined the long literary thoughts of a man on the night before the world was coming to an end. I wrote a number of tales like this forty-five years or so ago, not as predictions but as sometimes belabored warnings. In "Bonfire" my hero made lists of his great loves. Some of it ran like this:

"The thing that bothered William Peterson most was Shakespeare and Plato, and Aristotle, and Jonathan Swift and William Faulkner, and the poems of, well, Robert Frost, perhaps, and John Donne and Robert Herrick. All of these, mind you, tossed into the Bonfire. After that, he thought of bits of kindling (for that's what they would become), he thought of the massive

---

Michelangelo sculptures and El Greco and Renoir and on and on. For tomorrow they would all be dead, Shakespeare and Frost along with Huxley, Picasso, Swift and Beethoven, and his extraordinary library and quite ordinary self. . . ."

Not long after "Bonfire" I wrote a much more imaginative, I think, tale about the near future, "Bright Phoenix," in which a town librarian is threatened by the local patriot bigot in regard to a few dozen books aching to be burned. When the fire-makers arrive to kerosene the volumes, the librarian invites them in, and instead of stonewalling, uses somewhat subtle and absolutely obvious weapons to defeat them. As we move about the library and encounter the reading inhabitants therein, it becomes obvious that there is more behind their eyes and between their ears than might be guessed. As the Chief Censor burns books on the lawn outside the library, he takes coffee with the town librarian and speaks to a waiter in the cafe across the street, who comes with a steaming pot of coffee:

> "Hullo, Keats," I said.
> "Season of mists and mellow fruitfulness," said the waiter.
> "Keats?" said the Chief Censor. "His name isn't *Keats*!"
> "Silly," I said. "This is a Greek restaurant. Right, Plato?"
> The waiter refilled my cup. "The people have always some champion whom they set over them and nurse into greatness . . . this and no other is the root from which a tyrant springs; when he first appears, he is a protector."
> And, later, coming out of the restaurant, Barnes collided with an old man who almost fell. I grabbed his arm.
> "Professor Einstein," I said.
> "Mr. Shakespeare," he said.
> And as the library closes and a tall man exits, I say, "Good evening, Mr. Lincoln . . ."
> And he replies, "Four score and seven years—"

The book-burning town bigot, hearing this, realizes that the whole town has hidden books by memorizing them. There are books everywhere, hidden in people's heads! He goes mad, and the story finishes.

To be followed by more stories of a similar bent:

"The Exiles," concerning the characters in all the Oz and Tarzan and Alice books, and all the characters in the strange tales written by Hawthorne and Poe, exiled to Mars where one by one their ghosts melt and smoke and fly away to a final death when the last books on Earth are cremated.

In "Usher II" my hero collects all the intellectual book burners of Earth, those sad souls who believe fantasy is bad for the mind, dances them at a Red

Death costume ball, and sinks them to drown in a tarn as the second House of Usher vanishes from sight in countless fathoms.

Now for the fifth hop before the grand leap.

Some forty-two years ago, give or take a year, I was walking and talking with a writer friend in mid-Wilshire, Los Angeles, when a police car pulled up and an officer stepped out to ask what we were doing.

"Putting one foot in front of the other," I said, too much the smart-aleck.

That was the wrong answer.

The policeman repeated the question.

Too big for my britches, I replied, "Breathing the air, talking, conversing, walking."

The officer frowned. I explained:

"It's illogical, your stopping us. If we had wanted to burgle a joint or rob a shop, we would have driven up in a car, burgled or robbed, and driven away. As you see, we have no car, only our feet."

"Walking, eh?" said the officer. "Just walking?"

I nodded and waited for the obvious truth to sink in.

"Well," said the officer, "don't do it again!"

And the police car drove away.

Enraged by this Alice in Wonderland encounter, I ran home to write "The Pedestrian," concerning some future time when all walking was forbidden and all pedestrians treated as criminals. It was rejected by every magazine in the country and wound up in *The Reporter*, Max Ascoli's splendid political magazine, one of the best in the nation.

Thank God for that squad-car encounter, the curious questions, my half-dumb answers, for if I hadn't written "The Pedestrian" I might not, a few months later, have taken my midnight criminal stroller out for another jog around the city. When I did, what started as a word-or-idea association test turned into a 25,000-word novella entitled "The Fireman," which I had immense difficulty selling, for it was the time of the Un-American Activities Committee, run by J. Parnell Thomas, long before Joseph McCarthy arrived on the scene with Bobby Kennedy at his elbow for further hearings.

What about the library basement typing room and those nine dollars and fifty cents' worth of dimes with which I bought time and space in a room with a dozen other students at a dozen other typewriters?

Being relatively poor in 1950, I needed an office I couldn't afford. Wandering around the UCLA campus one noon, I heard typing sounds from below and went to investigate. With a glad cry I saw that it was indeed a rental typewriter typing room where, for ten cents a half-hour one could sit and create without the need of a proper office.

I sat, and three hours later realized I had been seized by an idea that started short but grew to wild size by day's end. The concept was so riveting I found it hard at sunset to flee the library basement and take the bus home to reality: my house, my wife, and our baby daughter.

I cannot possibly tell you what an exciting adventure it was, day after day, attacking that rentable machine, shoving in dimes, pounding away like a crazed chimp, rushing up stairs to fetch more dimes, running in and out of the stacks, pulling books, scanning pages, breathing the finest pollen in the world, book dust, with which to develop literary allergies. Then racing back down blushing with love, having found some quote here, another there to shove or tuck into my burgeoning myth. I was, like Melville's hero, madness maddened. I had no way to stop. I did not write *Fahrenheit 451—it* wrote *me*. There was a cycling of energy off the page, into my eyeballs, and around down through my nervous system and out through my hands. The typewriter and I were Siamese twins, joined at the fingertips.

It was a special triumph because I had been writing short stories from the age of twelve, through high school and into my thirties, thinking that I might never dare to leap off a cliff into a novel. Here, then, was the beginning of my daring to jump, without parachute, into a new form. Wild with enthusiasm for my rushing around the library, sniffing the bindings and relishing the inks, I soon found, as I have told you before, no one wanted "The Fireman." It was rejected by just about every magazine in the field and was finally published by *Galaxy* magazine, whose editor, Horace Gold, was braver than most in that time.

What caused my inspiration? There had to be a root system of influence, yes, that propelled me to dive headfirst into my typewriter and come up dripping with hyperbole, metaphor, and similes about fire, print, and papyrus.

Of course. There was Hitler torching books in Germany in 1934; rumors of Stalin and his match people and tinderboxes. Plus, long ago, the witch hunts in Salem in 1680, where my ten-times-great-grandmother Mary Bradbury was tried but escaped the burning. But most of it was my romantic background in Roman, Greek, and Egyptian mythology, starting at the age of three. Yes, three years old, three, when Tut was raised from his tomb and appeared in the weekend news gazettes in all his gold panoply, and I wondered what he was, and asked my folks!

So it was inevitable that I would hear or read about the triple burnings of the Alexandrian library, two of which were accidental, one on purpose. Knowing this at nine, I wept. For, strange child that I was, I was already an inhabitant of the high attics and haunted basements of the Carnegie Library in Waukegan, Illinois.

As I began, so I continued. There was nothing more wildly exciting than running to the library every Monday night when I was eight, nine, twelve, and fourteen, my brother running ahead to always win. Once inside, the old lady librarian (they were always old ladies in my childhood) weighed my books against my weight, and disapproving of the inequality (more books than boy) set me free to run home and lick the pages to turn them.

My madness continued as my family motored across country in 1932 and 1934 on Route 66. No sooner was our old Buick stopped than I was out and down the street to the nearest library where there must live different Tarzans, different Tik Toks, different Beauties and Beasts than the ones I knew.

Once out of high school, I could not afford college. I sold newspapers on a street corner for three years and inhabited the downtown library three or four days a week, often writing short stories on dozens of those small notepads strewn about libraries as a service to readers. I emerged from the library at the age of twenty-eight. Years later, during a lecture at a university, the president of the college, hearing of my total immersion in literature, presented me with a cap, cloak, and diploma and officially "graduated" me from the library.

Knowing I would be lonely and in need of further instruction, I took with me into life my poetry teacher and my short-story teacher from L.A. High. The latter, Jennet Johnson, died in her nineties only a few years ago, not long after inquiring as to my reading habits.

In the last forty years, I probably have written more poems, essays, stories, plays, and novels about libraries, librarians, and authors than any other writer today. I have written poems like "Emily Dickinson, Where Are You? Herman Melville Called Your Name Last Night in His Sleep." And another claiming Emily and Mr. Poe as my parents. And a story in which Charles Dickens moves into my grandparents' upstairs cupola room in the summer of 1932, calls me Pip, and allows me to collaborate on finishing *A Tale of Two Cities*. Finally, the library in *Something Wicked This Way Comes* is the pivotal meeting place at midnight for an encounter between Good and Evil, Mr. Halloway and Mr. Dark. All the women in my life have been teachers, librarians or booksellers. I found my wife, Maggie, in a bookshop in the spring of 1946.

But back to "The Fireman" and its fate once it was published in a pulp magazine. How did it grow to double its original size and move out into the world?

In 1953, two fine new things occurred. Ian Ballantine started a hard- and soft-cover venture, in which novels in both formats would be published on the same day. He saw in *Fahrenheit 451* the makings of a proper novel if I would add another 25,000 words to the first 25,000.

Could it be done? Remembering my investment of dimes and galloping up and downstairs from the UCLA stacks to the typing room, I feared for refiring the book and rebaking the characters. I am a passionate, not an intellectual, writer, which means my characters must plunge ahead of me to live the story. If my intellect caught up with them too swiftly, the whole adventure might mire down in self-doubt and endless mindplays.

The best answer was to set a deadline and ask Stanley Kauffmann, my Ballantine editor, to come to the coast in August. That would insure, I thought, this Lazarus book rising from the dead. This, plus conversations I was having in my head with the Fire Chief, Beatty, and the whole idea of future book burnings. If I could reignite him, let him stand and deliver his philosophy, no matter how cruel or lunatic, I knew that the book would shake itself awake to follow him.

I went back to the UCLA library, armed and weighted with a pound and a pint of ten-cent pieces to finish my "dime" novel. With Stan Kauffmann bearing down on me from the sky, I finished the last revised page in mid-August. I was ebullient. Stan cheered me on with *his* ebullience.

In the midst of which a phone call came that stunned us all. John Huston called, invited me to his hotel apartment, and asked if I would enjoy coming to Ireland for eight months in order to write the screenplay of *Moby Dick*. What a year, what a month, what a week.

I took the assignment, of course, leaving a scant few weeks later, with my wife and two daughters, to spend most of the next year overseas. Which meant hurrying to finish minor revisions on my fire brigade.

By this time we were deeply into the McCarthy period. McCarthy had bullied the Army into removing some "tainted" books from the overseas libraries. Former General, now President, Eisenhower, one of the few brave ones that year, ordered the books put back on the shelves. Meanwhile, our search for a magazine publisher to print portions of *Fahrenheit 451* came to a dead end. No one wanted to take a chance on a novel about past, present or future censorship.

It was then that the second great new thing occurred. A young Chicago editor, minus cash but full of future visions, saw my manuscript and bought it for four hundred and fifty dollars, all he could afford, to be published in issues number two, three, and four of his about-to-be-born magazine.

The young man was Hugh Hefner. The magazine was *Playboy*, which arrived during the winter of 1953–54 to shock and improve the world. The rest is history. From that modest beginning, a brave publisher in a frightened nation survived and prospered. When I saw Hefner at the opening of his new offices in California a few months ago, he shook my hand and said, "Thanks for being there." Only I knew what he was talking about.

There remains only to mention a prediction that my Fire Chief, Beatty, made in 1953, halfway through my book. It had to do with books being burned without matches or fire. Because you don't have to burn books, do you, if the world starts to fill up with nonreaders, nonlearners, nonknowers? If the world wide-screen-basketballs and -footballs itself to drown in MTV, no Beattys are needed to ignite the kerosene or hunt the reader. If the primary grades suffer meltdown and vanish through the cracks and ventilators of the schoolroom, who, after a while, will know or care?

All is not lost, of course. There is still time if we judge teachers, students, and parents, hold them accountable on the same scale, if we truly test teachers, students, and parents, if we make everyone responsible for quality, if we insure that by the end of its sixth year every child in every country can live in libraries to learn almost by osmosis, then our drug, street-gang, rape, and murder scores will suffer themselves near zero. But the Fire Chief, in mid-novel, says it all, predicting the one-minute TV commercial with three images per second and no respite from the bombardment. Listen to him, know what he says, then go sit with your child, open a book, and turn the page.

Well, then, at last what you have here is the love affair of a writer with the stacks; of a sad man, Montag, and his love affair not with the girl next door, but a knapsack of books. What a romance this is! The maker of lists in the "Bonfire" became the "Bright Phoenix" librarian who memorized Lincoln and Socrates, became "The Pedestrian" who walked late to become Montag, the man who smelled of kerosene, who met Clarisse who sniffed his uniform and told him his dreadful life function, which led Montag to show up in my typewriter one day forty years ago and beg to be born.

"Go," I said to Montag, thrusting another dime into the machine, "and live your life, changing it as you go. I'll run after."

Montag ran. I followed.

Montag's novel is here.

I am grateful that he wrote it for me.

RAFEEQ O. MCGIVERON

"To Build a Mirror Factory": The Mirror and Self-Examination in Ray Bradbury's "Fahrenheit 451"

Abstract: The mirror and self-examination are important in novelist Ray Bradbury's "Fahrenheit 451." All through the book Bradbury emphasizes the necessity of using a metaphorical mirror. Granger, the leader of the book-memorizing intellectuals, ties together the other mirror imagery, which appears throughout the book as mirrors of one kind are another are missed, found, seen, used. Self-examination is seen as a major part of avoiding self-destruction.

In *Fahrenheit 451* Ray Bradbury creates an unthinking society so compulsively hedonistic that it must be atom-bombed flat before it ever can be rebuilt. Bradbury's clearest suggestion to the survivors of America's third atomic war "started . . . since 1990" (73) is "to build a mirror factory first and put out nothing but mirrors . . . and take a long look in them" (164). Coming directly after the idea that they also must "build the biggest goddamn steam shovel in history and dig the biggest grave of all time and shove war in and cover it up" (164), the notion of the mirror factory might at first seem merely a throwaway line. Indeed, John Huntington suggests, with no little justification, that the whole passage is "confuse[d]" by its "vagueness, ambiguity, and misdirection" (138). Despite that, however, Bradbury shows throughout *Fahrenheit 451* the

From *Critique* 39, no. 3 (Spring 1998): pp. 282–287. © 1998 by Heldref Publications.

necessity of using a metaphorical mirror, for only through the self-examination
it makes possible can people recognize their own shortcomings.

The novel's first use of the mirror, a failed one, emphasizes the need for
self-examination. After a book burning, Guy Montag, the unsettled "fireman,"
knows "that when he return[s] to the firehouse, he might wink at himself, a
minstrel man, burnt-corked, in the mirror" (4). Montag's winking acceptance
of himself here is not reflective but reflexive, for his glance is superficial rather
than searching. Montag has the opportunity truly to examine himself, and if
he did, he might see a glorified anti-intellectual stormtrooper. However, the
situation, the surroundings, and even the mirror itself are too familiar, and he
does not see himself as he really is. Instead of recognizing the destructiveness
of his book-burning profession. his gaze is merely one of self-satisfaction.

Bradbury uses Clarisse, Guy's imaginative and perceptive seventeen-
year-old neighbor, as a metaphorical mirror to begin reflecting truths that
Montag otherwise would not see. The imagery of mirrors and reflection is
very clear:

> He saw himself in her eyes, suspended in two shining drops of
> bright water, himself dark and tiny, in fine detail, the lines about
> his mouth, everything there, as if her eyes were two miraculous
> bits of violet amber that might capture and hold him intact. (7)

Montag thinks of Clarisse again:

> How like a mirror . . . her face. Impossible, for how many people
> did you know who refracted your own light to you? . . . How rarely
> did other people's faces take of you and throw back to you your
> own expression, your own innermost trembling thought? (11)

William F. Touponce suggests that Montag thereby receives "a tranquil
affirmation of his being" (90); those passages bear that out.

But Clarisse's mirror imagery serves another function. Seeing himself
in the mirror of Clarisse helps Montag realize that he merely "[wears] his
happiness like a mask . . ." (12). He imagines that Clarisse has "run off across
the lawn with the mask . . ." (12). It would, however, be more accurate to
say that Montag himself throws away the poorly fitting mask after Clarisse
shows, or reflects to him, the truth underneath. Clarisse's game of rubbing a
dandelion under his chin to determine whether he is in love (21–2) "sum[s]
up everything" (44), showing Montag an aspect of his emptiness he otherwise
could not see. Her curiosity about why he and his wife have no children (28–9)
is another example of her mirror function. Perhaps most important, Clarisse
asks about Montag's job: "How did it start" How did you get into it? How

did you pick your work and how did you happen to think to take the job you have? . . . It just doesn't seem right for you, somehow" (23–4). With each little observation, game, or question, Clarisse reflects a previously unseen truth for Montag to examine and, in the words of Robert Reilly, "show[s] him how empty his existence is" (68).

In addition to serving as a mirror reflecting Montag himself, Clarisse also serves as a mirror held up to the rest of society. Her perspective helps Montag see that his contemporaries, as Clarisse says, really neither talk nor think about anything; "No, not anything. They name a lot of cars or clothes or swimming pools mostly and say how swell! But they all say the same things and nobody says anything different from anyone else" (31). That should be as familiar to Montag as the cloying stench of kerosene (of which Montag blithely observes, "You never wash it off completely" (61). Yet really to notice and examine those too-familiar facts he needs to see the situation reflected in the mirror of Clarisse.

Clarisse is a mirror not simply because she informs readers about the state of society. Each of the characters does that. If informing were the sole criterion for being a mirror. then even the most minor character would qualify—and so would most of the novel's narrative description. The metaphor would be so all-inclusive as to be meaningless. Clarisse is a mirror because she is so mirror-like in her informing. She "talk[s] about how strange the world is" (29), reminding Montag that "everyone . . . is either shouting or dancing around like wild or beating up one another" (30), but she has no ideological agenda. For the most part Clarisse does not interpret or offer suggestions; she merely draws Montag's attention to facts he should already understand but does not. Like a mirror, Clarisse guilelessly reflects the truth into Montag's eyes.

Guy's wife, Millie, is another mirror, although Bradbury has not set her up with imagery like Clarisse's. Like the firehouse mirror, however, she is such a part of Guy's routine that he cannot seem to see what she reflects. In the beginning of the novel, Guy may find it "a pleasure to burn" books (3) and may honestly claim that "kerosene . . . is nothing but perfume to me" (6), but Millie finds even more pleasure in the burning. She compulsively watches her three-wall television and begs Guy for a fourth wall that would cost one-third of his yearly salary (20–1). When not entranced by the television, she wears "thimble radios tamped tight" (12) in her ears, even in bed. Sometimes while her husband sleeps she drives all night out in the country, "feel[ing] wonderful" hitting rabbits and dogs (64). She has begun to overdose on sleeping pills but still maintains in bland disbelief, "I wouldn't do a thing like that" (18). Millie shows the superficiality and emptiness of the novel's society, yet Guy misses her miff or function. He finally recognizes her as "a silly empty woman" (44) who is "really bothered" (52), but he never seems to understand that she reflects an entire culture. As with the firehouse mirror, Montag has not looked carefully enough.

Beatty and Faber—chief book burner and former literature professor, respectively—both explain to Montag how the society of the past has turned into the inhumane world of *Fahrenheit 451*. Yet neither of those men is a mirror, for unlike Clarisse and Millie, they are overtly didactic. Each tries to sway Montag with a different interpretation of the past. Beatty wants Montag to "stand against the small tide of those who want to make everyone unhappy with conflicting theory and thought" (61–2), whereas Faber has no plans but at least wants Montag to think. Although the two characters provide important historical and sociological information, they are teachers more than mirrors. As Donald Watt notes, Beatty and Faber articulate the ideas that Millie and Clarisse live (197). They reflect society to some extent, but more often they evaluate and advise—tasks of the viewer and thinker, not the mirror.

The book contains other important mirrors. After a week of daily talks with Clarisse, Montag is ready to look into one of them. This time he takes more initiative, for the mirror is, one he must visualize himself. After ten years of simple acceptance, Montag finally sees himself by looking into the mirror of the other firemen:

> Montag looked at these men whose faces were sunburnt by a thousand real and ten thousand imaginary fires, whose work flushed their cheeks and fevered their eyes. These men who looked steadily into their platinum igniter flames as they lit their eternally burning black pipes. They and their charcoal hair and soot-colored brows and bluish-ash-smeared cheeks where they had shaven close. . . . Had he ever seen a fireman that didn't have black hair, black brows, a fiery face, and a blue-steel shaved but unshaved look? These men were all mirror images of himself! (33)

Montag is "appalled" (Watt 199), for this mirror invites a disquieting self-examination.

After looking into the ready-made mirror of Clarisse and recognizing an unflattering image mirrored by the other mindless firemen, Montag begins holding up his own mirror to society. The first attempt, when he and Millie look through the books he has stolen (66–74), is a comparative failure. Guy tells Millie, "[Books] just might stop us from making the same damn insane mistakes [people have always made]!" (74), but he cannot find a text that mirrors his own society clearly enough to provide either criticisms or solutions. Montag reads, "'It is computed that eleven thousand persons have at several times suffered death rather than submit to break their eggs at the smaller end'" (68). Swift's *Gulliver's Travels* may be, as Peter Sisario claims, "an excellent one for him to choose" (203), but it is excellent for the well-read reader, not for Montag. The firehouse mirror and the mirror that is Millie are missed opportunities because Montag does not look hard enough, but this book-mirror may be too subtle for him even to recognize.

Despite that failure, Professor Faber reminds Montag that mirrors are all around him. Although he does not speak in terms of mirrors, the idea of the reflection of truths fills his discussion:

> "It's not books you need, it's some of the things that once were in books. The same things could be in the [televised] parlor families' today. The same infinite detail and awareness could be projected through the radios and televisors, but are not. No, no, it's not the books at all you're looking for! Take it where you can find it, in old phonograph records, old motion pictures, and in old friends; look for it in nature and look for it in yourself. Books were only one type of receptacle where we stored a lot of things we were afraid we might forget. There is nothing magical in them at all. The magic is only in what the books say, how they stitched the patches of the universe together into one garment for us." (82–3)

Bradbury uses more than one type of imagery here, but the idea of the mirror could easily encompass them all. Throughout his talk Faber stresses examining the individual and society as reflected in a metaphorical mirror.

Faber says that books "can go under the microscope. You'd find life under the glass, streaming past in infinite profusion. The more pores, the more truthfully recorded details of life per square inch you can get on a sheet of paper, the more 'literary' you are" (83). Reiterating that idea, he says that books "show the pores in the face of life" (83). In other words, the microscope—or mirror—reflects important truths that otherwise would be missed. In that passage, Faber focuses on books; but his earlier discussion shows that a mirror can be found almost anywhere.

Finally, of course, Bradbury lets Montag stumble on a literary mirror that he, and even others, can recognize. When Guy reads Matthew Arnold's "Dover Beach" to Millie's friends, he holds up a mirror that reflects all too clearly:

> Ah, love, let us be true
> To one another! for the world, which seems
> To lie before us like a land of dreams,
> So various, so beautiful, so new,
> Hath really neither joy, nor love, nor light,

> Nor certitude, nor peace, nor help for pain;
> And we are here as on a darkling plain
> Swept with confused alarms of struggle and flight
> Where ignorant armies clash by night. (100)

Beatty calls American civilization "our happy world" (62), but families are hollow and loveless, suicide is commonplace, violence is endemic on the streets and in broadcast entertainment, and jet bombers circle ominously in the night. The poem's bleak conclusion rings so true that it makes the mindless Mrs. Phelps cry (100).

Just as Mrs. Phelps begins to get a glimmering of what it truly means to look in the mirror, Bradbury finally seems to allow Millie the same experience. As the bombs of one of the faceless enemies of an America that is "hated so much" abroad (74) begin to fall on the city from which he has fled, Guy's fancy conjures up a most significant image:

> Montag . . . saw or felt, or imagined he saw or felt the [television] walls go dark in Millie's face, heard her screaming, because in the millionth part of time left, she saw her own face reflected there, in a mirror instead of a crystal ball, and it was such a wildly empty face, all by itself in the room, touching nothing, starved and eating of itself that at last she recognized it as her own. (159–60)

Guy's peculiar little fantasy, of course, may not actually happen to Millie, but its existence demonstrates the crucial importance of the mirror. Unlike her husband, the imagined Millie of that passage recognizes its importance too late.

In the very last scene of the novel, Montag holds up the Bible as a mirror in which to see the world from a different perspective:

> And when it came his turn, what could he say. What could he offer on a day like this, to make the trip a little easier? To everything there is a season. Yes. A time to break down, and a time to build up. Yes. A time to keep silence, and a time to speak. Yes, all that. But what else? Something, something. . . . (165).

Ecclesiastes is a mirror providing some comfort, but Montag senses that Revelation is an even better one: "And on either side of the river was there a tree of life, which bare twelve manner of fruits, and yielded her fruit every month; And the leaves of the tree were for the healing of the nations" (165), Like Mrs. Phelps, he sees his own situation reflected in a piece of literature, but there the mirror brings hope rather than despair, without the mirror of the Bible, however, Montag would be hard pressed to see any positive "truths" in his postnuclear world.

Granger, leader of the book-memorizing intellectuals whom Montag meets after his flight from the city, ties together all the other uses of mirror imagery. "Come on now, we're going to build a mirror factory first and turn out nothing but mirrors for the next year and take a long took in them" (164). The suggestions reaffirms the necessity of using mirrors for self-examination. Just as Montag struggles to use figurative mirrors to discover the shortcomings in himself and in society, the survivors must use them in striving for a humane future. If they successfully use the mirrors, perhaps they can avoid making "the same damn mistakes."

Considered along with the other mirrors in *Fahrenheit 451*, Granger's suggestion begins to make metaphorical sense. Perhaps Bradbury's mirror imagery is not used as carefully as it could be; certainly it is possible to imagine its being more consistently employed or more fully articulated. Yet throughout the book, mirrors of a kind are missed and found, seen and used. With Montag's failures and successes, Bradbury shows that all of us, as individuals and as a society, must struggle to take a long, hard look in the mirror. Whether we look at ourselves from another's perspective or from the perspective of a good work of art, we need this self-examination to help avoid self-destruction.

Works Cited

Bradbury, Ray. *Fahrenheit 451*. 1953. New York: Ballantine, 1991.

Huntington, John. "Utopian and Anti-Utopian Logic: H.G. Wells and his Successors." *Science-Fiction Studies* 9 (1982): 122–46.

Reilly, Robert. "The Artistry of Ray Bradbury." *Extrapolation* 13 (1971): 64–74.

Sisario, Peter. "A Study of the Allusions in Bradbury's *Fahrenheit 451*." *English Journal* Feb. 1970: 200+.

Touponce, William F. "Ray Bradbury and the Poetics of Reverie." *Studies in Speculative Fiction 2*. 1981. Ann Arbor: UMI, 1984.

Watt, Donald A. "Burning Bright: *Fahrenheit 451* as Symbolic Dystopia." In *Ray Bradbury*. Writers of the 21st Century Series. Ed. Martin Harry Greenberg and Joseph D. Olander. New York: Taplinger, 1980. 195–213.

ROBIN ANNE REID

Fahrenheit 451 *(1953)*

*F*ahrenheit 451—the title refers to the temperature at which paper burns—
has its origin in Bradbury's earlier novella "The Fireman," published in *Galaxy*
in February 1951 (Eller "Finding List" 37). In a 1982 afterword, Bradbury
describes how he wrote the original novella in a basement typing room at the
library of the University of California at Los Angeles, where he could type for
half an hour for a dime. He finished the novella in nine days. When he took
breaks, he would walk through the stacks, enjoying the feel and smell of the
books. The importance of libraries, places maintained by governments that
contain books accessible to all, is at the heart of this novel.

The original novella was expanded (roughly doubled) into a novel,
Fahrenheit 451, published in 1953. François Truffaut adapted the novel for a
1966 film that Bradbury believes to be the best of the many film adaptations
of his work (Johnson, *Ray Bradbury* 139), and Bradbury himself adapted the
story for the Studio Theatre playhouse.

Fahrenheit 451 is considered one of Bradbury's best works. Like *The
Martian Chronicles*, it received praise from mainstream critics seldom accorded
those works published and marketed as "science fiction" during the 1950s. The
novel has been in print continuously, and has received a great deal of critical
attention from academics.

From *Ray Bradbury: A Critical Companion*, pp. 53–62. © 2000 by Robin Anne Reid.

Rafeeq McGiveron has published two academic essays on *Fahrenheit 451*: "What 'Carried the Trick': Mass Exploitation and the Decline of Thought in Ray Bradbury's *Fahrenheit 451*" discusses the issue of what caused the decline in society; readers and Bradbury himself tend to blame pressure from minority groups within society for the decline, but the text itself shows more of the blame belonging to mass culture. McGiveron's "'Do You Know the Legend of Hercules and Antaeus': The Wilderness in Ray Bradbury's *Fahrenheit 451*" analyzes the importance of the wilderness in the novel as both beautiful and optimistic but also humbling and powerful. Another scholar, Kevin Hoskinson in "*The Martian Chronicles* and *Fahrenheit 451*: Ray Bradbury's Cold War Novels" shows how both novels deal with social issues America faced during the Cold War years, especially "government oppression of the individual, the hazards of an atomic age, recivilization of society, and the divided nature of the 'Cold War Man'" (Hoskinson 346).

Susan Spencer, an academic critic who writes on literacy issues in science fiction, compares *Fahrenheit 451* with another dystopian novel, *A Canticle for Leibowitz* (1960) by Walter M. Miller, in a discussion of the way the two novels present the "post-apocalyptic library," the existence of an oral tradition, in which knowledge is handed down verbally, and a literate tradition, in which knowledge is written down. Diane Wood, in "Bradbury and Atwood: Exile as Rational Decision," compares *Fahrenheit 451* to Margaret Atwood's novel *The Handmaid's Tale* (1985) in their strongly political visions of a future mass culture in which reading is a heroic act. Mogen devotes a chapter to the novel, focusing on its satire of McCarthyism and its lyrical intensity.

PLOT DEVELOPMENT

Fahrenheit 451 is organized into three titled sections: "The Hearth and the Salamander," "The Sieve and the Sand," and "Burning Bright." The novel chronicles the protagonist's, Guy Montag's, change from acceptance of and pleasure in his job as a fireman, through his questioning of history and society, to his final rebellion against his job and country.

"The Hearth and the Salamander" describes events that begin Montag's transformation. The first event is his encounter with Clarisse McClellan, a seventeen-year-old neighbor who meets him late one night as he comes home after his shift. She asks him several questions, specifically what firemen used to do and whether he is happy. Montag tries to laugh off these questions, but the conversation reminds him of a meeting he had a year before with an unnamed old man, whom he later comes to know as Faber. When he enters his house and goes into the bedroom he shares with his wife, he finds she has attempted suicide. While the emergency team he calls pumps her stomach and replaces her blood, he thinks about her other suicide attempts. The third event is when the firemen are called to burn a collection of books owned by an old woman who chooses to burn with her books rather than leave.

The fourth event is Clarisse's death; she is killed in a hit-and-run accident, a common event that is not investigated as a crime. As a result, Montag feels ill and does not want to return to work. Chief Beatty comes to talk to Montag, giving him information about firemen, the official story of how their job evolved, and how important the firemen are in protecting society. Montag is not convinced. He shows Mildred the books he has been hiding for a year, ever since his first conversation with Faber in the park.

In the second section, "The Sieve and the Sand," Montag tries to explain his new ideas to the people around him. He first tries to talk with Mildred about the possibility of war, but she invites her friends over to watch the televisor, a combination virtual-reality room and television, reminiscent of the nursery in "The Veldt." Montag then goes to Faber, whose address he had from their first talk, with one of the books he rescued, the Bible. Faber gives Montag a different sense of history than Beatty's version. He tells Montag that there are three things missing from Montag's—and everyone's—life: the quality information or details that exists in good books, leisure time, and "the right to carry out actions based on what we learn from the interaction of the first two" (85). What has taken the place of these things is the superficial information put out on the televisor and "off-hours," which Faber insists are not the same as leisure.

Faber and Montag try to work out some means of resisting the firemen, or some other way of bringing back the forbidden books. Faber is afraid, but Montag forces him to agree to help by threatening to destroy the Bible. Faber knows a printer and agrees to work with Montag to set up an underground press. When Montag leaves, he has a radio through which Faber can talk to him.

Instead of pursuing the plan to set up a press, Montag returns home and tries to convince Mildred and her friends to question their views and read books. He reads them Matthew Arnold's poem "Dover Beach," but all three women respond angrily. Mildred tries to make up a cover story about how the firemen are allowed to bring one book home to share with their families as long as they incinerate it afterwards, and Montag does incinerate the book. Montag leaves the women and goes to the firehouse to confront Captain Beatty and the other firemen. While he's arguing with the captain, a call comes in, and they all go. When they arrive at the address, it's Montag's house, and he learns the call was made by Mildred.

The third section, "Burning Bright," describes Beatty giving Montag the choice of burning his own house and the books. The Mechanical Hound is present to enforce the burning. Montag does burn his house, but also burns Beatty and the Hound. Montag finds four books Mildred had missed, then escapes. He takes the books and hides them in one of firemen's house and calls in an alarm, then goes to Faber's house. Faber tells him that war has been declared, and they watch a televised chase by another Mechanical Hound. They decide to try to cover Montag's scent, and Faber decides to leave the city for St. Louis. After a long chase, Montag makes it to the river and floats to freedom.

As he makes his way through a wilderness that surrounds the city, he meets a group of men who have formed an underground movement to remember books. They help him by giving him a potion to change his body chemistry, or scent, and show him how the televised hunt for him resulted in an innocent man's death. As they are talking the next day, they hear jets overhead and hear bombs destroying the city. At the end, the men are walking north, planning to wait out the war and then start a movement to write and make their books available.

CHARACTER DEVELOPMENT

Guy Montag is the novel's protagonist and its main point of view character. He is the only character whose thoughts and emotions are described for the reader (other than a couple of short sections that report the Mechanical Hound's point of view). Since the major focus of the book is Montag's transformation from a dedicated fireman to a participant in an underground library movement, the use of the third-person perspective allows the reader to follow Montag's development, witnessing how he responds to the events and characters around him.

The opening section is a scene from Montag's point of view. This section does not use Montag's name and is primarily composed in the passive voice, a sentence structure that denies that any subject has agency, or the power to act. The first line of the novel is "It was a pleasure to burn" (3). The lack of a name and the passive voice constructs Montag as representative of all firemen, anonymous, focused on the pleasure inherent in the process of destroying books, houses, and people.

Montag begins to question his life and society and comes to the realization that neither he nor his wife Mildred are happy. His unhappiness is shown by his hiding of forbidden books, and her unhappiness surfaces in regular attempts to commit suicide. Montag begins to wonder why he is unhappy. By the end of the novel, Montag has become an active participant who has claimed his own agency; leading a group of men through the wilderness, he recites part of what he has memorized from the Bible. Planning to share his "book" with his fellow "librarians," Montag begins to take on the status of a leader, someone who is planning a better future.

The other characters in the novel serve as either catalysts or supporters for Montag or as antagonists who work against him, and are described in terms of the effect they have on him. The characters Clarisse and Faber contribute most to his change and support him, while Mildred and Captain Beatty oppose his attempts to change and become his antagonists.

The same characters interact with Montag throughout the novel. He is influenced by Clarisse's disappearance, Mildred's addiction to the "TV parlor," or televisor, and Faber's own attempts to resist the socially driven destruction of all books, as well as people who try to save books. Pressure from the Fire Chief and Captain Beatty and the ongoing announcements of war that punctuate the novel also contribute to Montag's change.

Montag's prominence as the protagonist results in a greater narrative focus on his development as a character than is the case for the other characters. What he thinks about his marriage and wife Mildred, his sense that they have both lost something (which Mildred denies when he tries to talk to her about it), his fear of the Mechanical Hound, his attraction to Clarisse, as well as his childhood memories and perceptions of the men he works with all create a characterization with emotional depth. Other characters' actions and speech are described, but no information on their thoughts or feelings is given.

The reasons why other characters do what they do is not as clear, but their effect on Montag is described. Clarisse and Faber have important conversations with Montag that cause him to doubt his social function and way of life. Clarisse, a young woman who lives with her family near Montag, likes to do things most people consider crazy: walk at night; talk about happiness, love, and nature; and question what is presented as normal or socially appropriate. The other character who supports Montag in his changing ideas is Faber, a retired English professor, who has been trying to work out a solution to the book burnings on his own. He has not moved to active resistance because, as he tells Montag, he's a coward. One of the main functions Faber serves in the novel is to answer some of Montag's questions and to give him ideas for how to change what he is doing. Faber shelters Montag from the Mechanical Hound and helps him escape to the countryside, where he meets an underground resistance movement, consisting of mostly philosophy and literature professors who are remembering books that they hope to write down after the war.

Two characters in the novel serve as antagonists and represent the larger antagonist in the novel, American society: Mildred and Captain Beatty. Mildred, Montag's wife, is addicted to the televised mass culture provided nonstop; she sees the characters in her programs as more real than her husband. However, her unacknowledged unhappiness with her life is shown by regular suicide attempts. After Clarisse's disappearance, Montag challenges Mildred. After one conversation, Montag brings out books he's been hiding for a year, since his first conversation with Faber. Mildred's first response is to try to cover up for him in some way, then to withdraw even further into her TV parlor; eventually, she turns him in. Mildred does not want to question society's reliance on technology and its choice to burn books. She does not remember her suicide attempts and denies that she is unhappy in any way.

Captain Beatty is a more active antagonist. Beatty represents the institutional or government voice, while Mildred is constructed as a consumer of the TV parlor's representation of the world. Beatty presents the official history of the firemen to Montag, but Beatty is also able to quote a great number of books and to recognize the source of something Montag had read. Beatty can quote Philip Sidney, Alexander Pope, Dr. Johnson, and a plethora of other authors not identified in the text (105–6) as he argues against Montag's desire to save and read books. The Fire Chief quotes books to prove that the texts contradict each other. His knowledge of books along with his position show that the government allows some people in power access to books as long as they remain dedicated to burning books owned by individuals. Chief Beatty finally pushes Montag to his limit, and Montag kills him.

SETTING

Fahrenheit 451 is set in an unnamed city in the United States, possibly in the Midwest, in some undated future. The sole geographical references are the fact that the city has a bus station where Faber can take a bus to St. Louis and Montag's memory of meeting his wife in Chicago. The only time referent is Montag's comment that the country has started two atomic wars since 1990. Within the city, certain locations are specified as important: Montag's house, which is in the suburbs, Faber's house, and the fire station where he works a night shift. At the end of the novel, Montag has escaped the city by means of a river and is traveling through a countryside, or wilderness, with other men, all of whom have memorized books and plan to write them down after the war has ended.

THEMES

Fahrenheit 451's major themes of resistance against the conformity imposed by a mass media and the use of technology to control individuals are linked to its depiction of a dystopia. As M. Keith Booker explains in *Dystopian Literature: A Theory and Research Guide*, one strategy dystopian literature takes is to criticize existing social and political systems by extending the premises of those systems to reveal their flaws (Booker 3). Much of the science fiction published in the 1940s and 1950s presented technology as a positive force and space travel as a happy prospect for humanity; at the same time, America was engaging in World War II, which led to the development of atomic bombs and to the Cold War. Both Hoskinson and Mogen have examined the extent to which *Fahrenheit*

451 criticizes McCarthyism and Cold War attitudes. The novel also criticizes American attitudes toward and dependence on technology.

Bradbury's main theme is the extent to which technology can be used for social control, specifically through the use of the mass media for all education and entertainment. The novel describes people being bombarded twenty-four hours a day by "TV class," "film teacher[s]," and TV parlors and televisors. The technology is used to promote a mass culture and to suppress individualism. American reliance on the automobile is also singled out as a major problem, with Clarisse being killed in a hit-and-run accident, Mildred driving fast in the country and killing animals when she is depressed, and Montag himself nearly being killed by a group of teenagers in a car.

The dystopian future in the novel is also created by the social control of history and knowledge, enforced through the technology of book burning. Since access to printed knowledge and books is restricted, the only source for information is the government, which presents a distorted and simplified view of history. The government is not the only cause of this future: Beatty and Faber claim that the American population, in its desire for positive images and simplicity, demanded the suppression of books as complex, contradictory, and difficult. Beatty tends to blame "minority groups" such as specific religions, ethnic minorities, professional groups—anyone who objected to depictions in books. Faber insists that the "public itself stopped reading of its own accord. [The] firemen provide a circus now and then at which buildings are set off and crowds gather for the pretty blaze, but it's a small sideshow indeed and hardly necessary to keep things in line" (87).

While some dystopias (such as George Orwell's *1984* [1949]) put all the responsibility for oppression on the government, Bradbury's novel does not show the national government acting in any way, with the exception of periodic references to planes flying overhead with bombs. Only after most Americans chose to give up reading, seduced by the simplicity and presence of the mass media, did the government step in. As McGiveron argues in "What 'Carried the Trick,'" Bradbury's novel is more an indictment of mass culture than of a specific system of government.

ALTERNATIVE PERSPECTIVE:
A STYLISTIC READING

One way of analyzing a literary work is called stylistic analysis. This sort of analysis looks closely at how a writer chooses and arranges words. A stylistic analysis can focus on the author's choice of words, grammar, or syntax (sentence structure). Usually a stylistic analysis will focus on one kind of stylistic choice (such as images) or, if on a variety of choices, on a fairly short excerpt from the work. Stylistic analysis always considers how the style contributes to the work's theme or the overall meaning.

Images are words that evoke sensory impressions: touch, taste, smell, sight, hearing. Images provide a sense of the physical reality a character experiences in a story. In realistic fiction, images are not necessarily foregrounded, that is, given a great deal of attention. Such images often serve more as background information, meant to be taken literally for their descriptive value. But in other genres, images take on the importance they have in poetry: that is, they sometimes act as symbols, with abstract or thematic meanings as well as a literal or descriptive meaning. The term "image cluster" is used when a writer builds in a number of references to a core image.

Bradbury uses images associated with fire and burning as well as images of light and running water, throughout *Fahrenheit 451*. The novel's reliance on a specific pattern of images is discussed in detail by Donald Watt in "'Fahrenheit 451' as Symbolic Dystopia." Watt provides a careful description and analysis of how these images are associated with important characters and events throughout the novel. Images used to describe events or characters make the novel a "symbolic dystopia" for Watt, with the stylistic choices Bradbury makes resulting in a subtle and distinctive dystopian novel. Watt shows how Bradbury's use of fire imagery, with fire as both negative and positive, sets up two symbolic poles (196).

A stylistic reading can show how Bradbury brings together his three major image clusters in a short passage near the end of the novel. At this point in the story, Montag has escaped a Mechanical Hound by going into the river. Floating downstream, he is thinking about his life and the choices he has made. He previously planned to take violent action against the firemen, and has killed Captain Beatty. But after this passage, he decides not to destroy or burn anything else. Instead, he will try to preserve knowledge and life:

> He saw the moon low in the sky now. The moon there, and the light of the moon caused by what? By the sun of course. And what lights the sun? Its own fire. And the sun goes on, day after day, burning and burning. The sun and time. The sun and time and burning. Burning. The river bobbled him along gently. Burning. The sun and every clock on the earth. It all came together and became a single thing in his mind. After a long time of floating on the land and a short time of floating in the river he knew why he must never burn again in his life. (140–41)

This passage has 112 words, arranged in thirteen sentences, although six of those sentences are fragments (lacking either a subject or a verb). Little action takes place: Montag is floating, passively, in the river. He sees and, by the end, he knows. The river is what moves him ("bobbled him along gently"). Since the passage lacks action verbs or, in some sentences, any verbs, the nouns attract greater attention: there are twenty-eight noun phrases, including verbals, the -ing forms of verbs, which can function as nouns or modify nouns. (There are also two verbs, "lights" and "burns" which closely parallel similar nouns.) One-quarter of the words in this passage, then, are in noun phrases.

The nouns are mostly related to Bradbury's image clusters: *sun* is used six times; *fire* and *light* are each used once. The verbal *burning* is used five times. *Moon* is used three times, and closely associated with the sun (its light comes from the sun), and *sky* is used once. *River* is used twice, and *land* and *the earth* once. The contrasting images of burning (of fires and of the sun) are brought together with the water of the river and the land. The moon, "low in the sky," is nearly touching the land, and it connects the light of the sun with the earth and water. "It all" becomes "a single thing" to Montag. The other major image cluster is related to time: *time* occurs four times, *day* twice, and *clock* once. The passing of time is paralleled with the sun in two sentences: "The sun and time. The sun and time and burning."

The images in this passage have all been used before, throughout the novel, to describe characters and events, and Montag's perceptions of them. This view of the universe, in which the opposing or destructive forces meld with the nurturing or creative forces, is a vision that results in Montag's decision to move away from destruction, even destruction for a "good cause," and toward preservation. Described in a deceptively simple style, these perceptions lead him to a new consciousness and a final decision on how he should live his life from this point on. After he leaves the river, he shortly joins the underground resistance group and commits to joining their project of memory and preservation.

GEORGE E. CONNOR

Spelunking with Ray Bradbury: The Allegory of the Cave in Fahrenheit 451

According to Holtsmark, "for reasons of plot, character, and allusion, among others, myth is a central feature of ancient Greek literature, [and] it has appeared tacitly axiomatic from the time of antiquity that myth informs most narrative literature" (2001, 24). Greek authors turned to myth "at those crucial points at which pure reason seem[ed] unable to advance further" (Kirk 1970, 259). Foremost among the mythic themes in Greek literature is the word *katabasis*, which "literally means 'a going down, a descent,' capturing the imagined physical orientation of the other world relative to this one" (Holtsmark 25). Obvious manifestations of this theme can be found in the Homeric journeys of the *Odyssey* (1996) and the *Iliad* (1991). In both books, Homer utilizes physical caves to accent the literary descent. Although he rejected certain literary applications of myth, especially among the poets, Plato "reasserted the role of myth in his own practice" (Kirk 1970, 250). In particular, Plato asserted the role of myth in the dialogue of the *Republic* when "reason seemed unable to advance further."

The *katabasis* tradition is introduced into the *Republic* at the beginning of Book VII when Socrates asks Glaucon to "make an image of our nature in its education and want of education, likening it to a condition of the following kind. See human beings as though they were in an underground cave-like dwelling" (1968, 514a). This passage is the opening line of Plato's Allegory of

From *Extrapolation* 45, no. 4 (Winter 2004): pp. 408–418. © 2004 by the University of Texas at Brownsville and Texas Southmost College.

the Cave. With little question, scholars agree that the Allegory "is the keystone of the dialogue" (Sandoz 1971, 62). The textual relevance of the Allegory for Ray Bradbury's *Fahrenheit 451* is obvious in Montag's hope that "maybe the books can get us half out of the cave" (1953, 74). Perhaps less obvious, the following analysis demonstrates that Plato's Allegory is the central metaphor for the novel. More specifically, the Allegory provides a template by which Bradbury's characters can be analyzed and distinguished.

Initially, this analysis rests upon the explicit linkage between literature and political philosophy. With respect to literature, Zuckert insists that novels can be "forms of political thought" (1990, ix). Reflecting her subtitle, *Political Philosophy in Novel Form*, Zuckert examines the perspective of the author and suggests, "novelists' often differing theoretical reflections have led them nevertheless to agree on the need for literary political teaching" (ix). With respect to the audience, she suggests that "aware of readers' antipathy to arguments by authority, novelists appeal to readers' own experience by enlisting their sympathies through empathetic identification with the protagonists of the stories" (247). Complementing Zuckert's view, Strauss maintains that "[t]he study of the literary question is an important part of the study of what philosophy is" (1964, 52). Using *Fahrenheit 451* as an example, science fiction author Frederik Pohl similarly argues "there is very little science fiction, perhaps no good science fiction at all, that is not to some degree political" (1997, 7). The linkage between the two fields rests upon the fact that "political theorists and science fiction writers alike are continually aware of the role of language" (Hassler and Wilcox 1997, 1).

With respect to language, the significance of metaphor is probably the single most analyzed aspect of Bradbury's fiction: Mogen (1986), Watt (1980, 2000), McNelly (1980), Mengeling (1980), Wolfe (1980) McGiveron (1996), and Sisario (1970). Scholarly attraction to the concept is best explained by McNelly: "For Bradbury, a metaphor is not merely a figure of speech, it is a vital concept, a method he uses for comprehending one reality and expressing it in terms of another; it permits the reader to perceive what the author is saying" (1982). Nevertheless, for all the attraction to the concept, whether scholars use the term metaphor, imagery, symbol, or, like Mogen, allegory, they do not discuss *the* Allegory. Only Pell (1980), who links Bradbury's imagery to Aristotle, and Spencer (1999), who discusses Bradbury in the context of Plato's *Phaedrus*, address Bradbury's relationship to his ancient Greek predecessors. However, neither Pell nor Spencer link Bradbury or *Fahrenheit 451* to Plato's Allegory.

Finally, the present application of the Allegory is rooted in Morson's (1981) discussion of "combined genres" and his delineation of the utopian "masterplot." Like Zuckert, Morson argues that writers "exploit an audience's favorable disposition" (95) and exploit the "readers' willingness to think in unfamiliar or nonhabitual ways" (94). However, unlike Zuckert's broader discussion of novels, Morson narrows his application to a discussion of a more particular genre. Although he admits that he is not concerned with "defining" (ix), Morson initially labels *Fahrenheit 451* as "anti-utopia" (117). Later, he settles on dystopia: "Whereas utopias invite their readers to contemplate a world in which they would at last be at home, dystopias invite their readers to contemplate one in which they would have 'no place' at all" (141–142). Morson concludes that "combined genres are not in principle incompatible" and "it is quite possible to read *Fahrenheit 451* as both science fiction and anti-utopia" (117). Broadening the idea of "combined genres" a bit further, Sargent proposes a more inclusive definition that encompasses both "anti-utopia," or dystopian, literature and utopian literature: "Whatever we label these works—be it utopias, social science fiction, or tales of the future—they are part of the utopian tradition since they do present fairly detailed descriptions of nonexistent social systems" (1975, 144). This approach allows scholars to avoid the tangle of definition and classification so evident in the literature on *Fahrenheit 451* (Reid 2000, 7–13).

Definitional questions aside, it is Morson's application of the Allegory that undergirds his analysis. Although earlier scholarship linked Dostoevsky to the Allegory (Sandoz 1971, xiv), Morson broadened this linkage to suggest that Plato's Allegory, as well as the counterplots of "the madman" and "escape," provide the "masterplot" for the entire genre of utopian fiction (38). He maintains "most utopias describe a similar journey from darkness to light, followed by a real or imagined return" (89). With specific reference to dystopias, Morson notes that because "[a]n anti-generic work must parody a target genre," the *Republic* serves as a "negative model" for *Fahrenheit 451*. However, Morson's reference to *Fahrenheit 451* is related to Plato's "suspicion of poetry" and not specifically to the Allegory. Whereas Morson could not, in a single volume, address the myriad applications of his theory, this analysis reexamines and expands Morson's theory in a character-driven discussion of Bradbury's *Fahrenheit 451*.

In short, Bradbury's *Fahrenheit 451* provides a venue for an interdisciplinary examination of the linkage between literature and philosophy, the concept of metaphor, and the application of a unifying theory that places the book into a broader context.

THE ALLEGORY

Morson's delineation of the Allegory is limited to the "masterplot" and the counterplots of "the madman" and "escape." While this three-part discussion was adequate for Morson's purpose and consistent with what is defined as "the thematic simplicity, almost shallowness, of most Greek myths (Kirk

1970, 187), the discussion below is based upon a six-part division that focuses specifically on the cave's inhabitants: Those who are bound in the cave; the cave's puppeteers; the madman; those who escape from the cave; those who help the escapees; and those who would return to the cave.

The Allegory begins with those who are bound in the cave. "They are in it from childhood with their legs and necks in bonds so that they are fixed, seeing only in front of them," seeing nothing "other than the shadows cast by the fire on the side of the cave facing them" (514a,b, 515a). Socrates concludes that "such men would hold that the truth is nothing other than the shadows of artificial things" (515c). Behind those who are bound are the cave's puppeteers. "Human beings carrying all sorts of artifacts, which project above the wall, and statues of men and other animals wrought from stone, wood and every kind of material; as is to be expected, some of the carriers utter sounds while others are silent" (514c, 515a). Third, is the component that Morson identifies as the "madman" subplot: "[i]f they were somehow able to get their hands on and kill the man who attempts to release and lead up, wouldn't they kill him?" (517a).

The next distinction is the one Morson labels as the "escape." "[I]f someone dragged him away from there by force along the rough, steep, upward way and didn't let him go before he had dragged him out into the light of the sun" (515e). The discussion below divides this escape into two parts. Morson focuses on the reaction of the person being dragged up. If they were "release[d] from bonds and folly" and "compelled to stand up, to turn his neck around, to walk and look up toward the light." Socrates argued that he would be "distressed" and this would all be done "in pain because he is dazzled," and he would "be unable to see even one of the things now said to be true" (515c, 515e, 516a). While the reaction is important, a character-driven analysis should also consider the "someone" who does the dragging. This "someone" is described by Bloom as a "guide" (1968, 403). The final aspect of the Allegory consists of the return to the cave. Here again, this analysis departs from Morson by subdividing the "madman" subplot. When faced with the choice of returning to the shadows of the cave, Glaucon concludes that the former inhabitant of the cave "would prefer to undergo everything rather than live that way" (516d).

Morson argues, "works of this highly determined genre repeat that plot, either in part or in its entirety." The discussion below examines how Bradbury's *Fahrenheit 451* repeats the six parts of the Allegory in their entirety. Touponce noted "the complaint that utopian novels are more concerned with ideas than characters, and present characters who are simply one-dimensional spokesmen the author's social hypothesis, is often voiced." He concluded that, "this charge [cannot] be brought successfully against Fahrenheit 451" (1984, 110). For example, scholars have explored the multi-dimensionality of Montag.

Hoskinson discusses "Montag's liberation from Captain Beatty" (1995, 345). Similarly, but perhaps a bit more philosophical, Zipes maintains that Montag "begins to assume command of his own destiny" (2000, 131). Nevertheless, a narrow focus on Montag's evolution from cave dweller/puppeteer to guide, although reasonably within the metaphor of the cave, diminishes the literary value of Bradbury's other characters. While the number of named and un-named characters is not large, each one finds his or her own place in the Allegory.

ALLEGORICAL APPLICATION

Amis maintains, "Bradbury's is the most skillfully drawn of all science fiction's conformist hells" (2000, 96). Montag's conformist colleagues find themselves bound in the cave and testifying to shadows in response to Montag's question about the history of firemen. "Stoneman and Black drew forth their rule books, which also contained brief histories of the Fireman of America." "Established, 1790, to burn English-influenced books in the Colonies. First Fireman: Benjamin Franklin" (34). While Stoneman and Black acknowledge the shadows they have been shown, Montag's wife, Mildred, epitomizes Socrates' conclusion that the inhabitants of the cave "would hold that the truth is nothing other than the shadows of artificial things." Mildred has her sleeping tablets (13), electric bees (18), seashell (42), and thimble (48). Most importantly, Mildred has her "walls" (44). Here she has her own "part" (20) in a fictional "family" (77). Here, "Three White Cartoon Clowns chopped off each other's limbs to the accompaniment of immense incoming tides of laughter" (94). Mildred has become so engrossed in her shadow "family" that she cannot remember when she and Montag met and concludes, "it doesn't matter" (43).

Captain Beatty is the best single character to represent the "human beings carrying all sorts of artifacts." Unlike those bound in the cave, these puppeteers know that the figures on the wall are mere "shadows of artificial things." In short, the puppeteers know the truth about the cave and Beatty knows the truth about the world around him. He is both a representative of the "exploiters" (McGiveron 1996, 249) and a defender of "a consumer culture completely divorced from political awareness" (Seed 1994, 228). Unlike Stoneman and Black, the Captain knows the secret history of their profession and he tells Montag, "I'll let you in on it" (54). Quoting Dr. Johnson, he tells Montag, both in a dream and in person, "He is no wise man that will quit a certainty for an uncertainty" (106). And Beatty knows the certainties. They are defined in people like Mildred. The certainties of this world are 3-D sex magazines, sex, heroin, and noncombustible data (57–58, 61).

A casual reading of the text might suggest that Guy Montag fulfills the role of Morson's "madman." The real and televised pursuit of Montag is illustrative of the inhabitants of the cave rising up against one "who attempts to release and lead up." "Police alert. Wanted: Fugitive in city. Has committed murder and crimes against the State. Name: Guy Montag. . . . watch for a man alone, on foot" (124). However, Montag lives. A more intriguing illustrator of the madman subplot would be Clarisse McClellan. Unlike the drivers racing down the highways, Clarisse knew what grass, flowers, and dew were (9). She let raindrops fall on her face (21) and she "smelled old leaves" (29). Montag exclaims, "She saw everything. She didn't do anything to anyone" (114). This statement is, of course, untrue because Clarisse's "madness" was to go down into the cave and lead Montag up. Her eventual fate, however, is something that Bradbury only gradually reveals. At first, Montag simply notices that "Clarisse was gone" (32). Later, Mildred suggests that she was "[r]un over by a car." "I don't know. But I think she's dead" (47).

With Montag unable to remember her face, Captain Beatty intones that the "poor girl's better off dead" (60). It is not until the final confrontation between Beatty and Montag, that a more sinister end is suggested. Catching Montag's wistful glance "Beatty snorted." "Oh, no! You weren't fooled by that little idiot's routine, were you?" (113). "She chewed you around, didn't she? One of those damn do-gooders with their shocked, holier-than-thou silences, their talent making others feel guilty" (114). Although Bradbury does not make it explicit, the text suggests that, unlike the "madman" Montag, who lives, the "madman" Clarisse is killed by the inhabitants of the cave (Sisario 1970, 203; Hoskinson 1995, 348).

Although the death of the "madman" is a significant component of the Allegory, Plato's text does allow for the successful release of the cave's inhabitants. Here this analysis turns to the "someone" who drags the inhabitant "into the light of the sun." The choice of illustrative characters, Faber and Granger, is fairly simple. Faber admits that "we do need knowledge" (86) but he is initially reluctant to join Montag. Later, he continues the work of Clarisse by helping Montag escape. In the novel, Faber helps Montag escape from the police. In the metaphor, he helps Montag escape from the cave. "I feel like I'm doing what I should've done a lifetime ago. For a little while I'm not afraid. Maybe it's because I'm doing the right thing at last" (131). Continuing the work of Faber, and helping Montag on his journey out of the city and out of the cave is Granger. Their world, their cave, had been destroyed in an instant. In the aftermath, there would be "a lot of lonely people" (164). These survivors would be trying to find their own path "along the rough steep, upward way." Granger and his companions "can be of some use in the world" (152) by leading them into the light. Strauss argues, "the *Republic* never abandons the fiction that the just city as a society of human beings is possible" (1964, 129). While Granger thinks they "will win out in the long run," the text also suggests that he has his doubts about the future of humanity: "But even when we had the books on hand, a long time ago, we didn't use what we got out of them. We went right on insulting the dead. We went right on spitting in the graves of all the poor ones who died before us" (164). Bloom maintains that the one who drags people out of the cave and into the light "can only lead a few" (1968, 403). Similarly Granger argues that "[w]e pick up a few more people every generation" (163).

Socrates maintains that the person dragged into the light of the sun would be "distressed" (515e). Jowett (Plato 1948) translates this passage as "suffer sharp pains." The conflict between truth and shadow in *Fahrenheit 451* is equally painful. When confronted by Montag, Faber exclaims, "I care so much I'm sick." This same physical distress is revealed when Montag's reading of *Dover Beach* struck a long-buried nerve in Mrs. Phelps. "She sobbed uncontrollably" and "her faced squeezed itself out of shape" (100). These examples notwithstanding, it is Montag himself who best illustrates the physical dimensions of facing the truth. After burning the unnamed neighbor of Mrs. Blake, Montag "had chills and fever in the morning" (48) and "suddenly the odor of kerosene made him vomit" (49). Thrust into moderating a debate between Faber and Beatty, his "head whirled sickeningly" (107). Just before the death of Beatty, Montag feels an earthquake "shaking and falling and shivering inside him and he stood there, his knees half bent under the great load of tiredness and outrage" (118). After Beatty's death, "Montag kept his sickness down long enough" (120).

The choice of characters representing those "would prefer to undergo everything rather than live that way" is, in one case, textually obvious. The unnamed neighbor of Mrs. Blake didn't simply die in the firemen's inferno; she committed suicide. She would not be forced to live in a world that contained only shadows. "The woman on the porch reached out with contempt to them all and struck the kitchen match against the railing" (40). Montag himself suggests the second example of refusing to go back into the cave: "Beatty wanted to die" (122). In the climatic scene between Beatty and Montag, Beatty's can no longer bear the role of puppeteer. In fact, Beatty dares Montag to kill him: "There is no terror, Cassius, in your threats, for I am arm'd so strong in honesty that they pass me as an idle wind which I respect not." "Go ahead now, you second-hand litterateur, pull the trigger" (119). In the end, Faber's thought that Beatty "could be one of us" (91) was closer to the truth than either he or Montag ever imagined.

CONCLUSION

Kirk suggests that Greek myths "can hardly be understood in isolation" (v). As the discussion above demonstrates, the same should be said about Ray Bradbury's *Fahrenheit 451*. While Plato's Allegory of the Cave is the defining metaphor for *Fahrenheit 451*, it must be recognized that the Allegory itself is part of the larger *katabasis* tradition and that that tradition is itself part of an even larger tradition in Greek literature. Kirk maintains "the detailed study of mythical themes in the literature of the classical period in Greece is essential for the understanding of the whole culture" (1). This analysis suggests that a detailed study of the mythical themes in *Fahrenheit 451* is essential for the understanding of Bradbury. Moreover, by examining the linkage between literature and philosophy, the role of metaphor, and the application of Morson's theory, this analysis transcends traditional disciplinary boundaries.

Khanna's asserts that the "disjunction between theory and praxis, literature and politics, art and life, or text and body is exactly what the utopian enterprise denies" (39). Keeping in mind Sargent's inclusive approach to the "utopian enterprise," this analysis suggests that Bradbury's *Fahrenheit 451* provides ample evidence for Khanna's assertion on all counts. While one could analyze the relationship between theory and praxis, art and life, and text and body within the novel, *Fahrenheit 451* best exemplifies the conjunction of literature and politics as defined by the literary theories of Zuckert and Strauss. Moreover, *Fahrenheit 451* illustrates the centrality of the role of language in the science fiction genre.

Bradbury's use of metaphor is, as was demonstrated above, central to the role of language in *Fahrenheit 451*. In the same way that Plato inserted myth into the *Republic*, Bradbury borrowed the "masterplot" of the Allegory of the Cave. In substituting metaphor for reason, like Plato, Bradbury may have sought to "replace opinion about the nature of political things by the knowledge of the nature of political things" (Strauss 1959, 11–12). There is, however, one key difference between Bradbury's cave and Plato's cave. In assessing the Platonic model, Strauss insists, "the *Republic* never abandons the *fiction* that the just city as a society of human beings is possible" [emphasis added]. Strauss argues that "[t]he just city is impossible. It is impossible because it is against nature. It is against nature that there should ever be a 'cessation of evils'" (1964, 129; 127). Unlike Strauss, Bradbury has hope for a "cessation of evils" and, unlike Plato's *Republic*, *Fahrenheit 451* was not constructed solely for contemplation.

According to Bloom's analysis of the *Republic*, "[t]he philosopher does not bring light to the cave, he escapes into the light and can lead a few to it; he is a guide, not a torchbearer" (1968, 403). Consistent with Bloom's analysis, Faber, Granger and Montag serve as Platonic guides in the text and, in fact, only lead a few to the light. Regardless of the role of these characters *in the text*, it can be demonstrated that *through the text* Bradbury himself relished the role of torchbearer in his quest to lead the cave dwellers to enlightenment. Here, again, Morson's theory helps to define the voice of the author in utopian fiction.

If, as was argued above, neither Montag nor any other single character is a spokesman for the author, how is the author's voice revealed? Morson inquires, "[i]nasmuch as literary utopias are either entirely or mostly fictional, and the 'fictional contract' suspends authorial responsibility for statements represented rather than made, it may be asked how is it possible to say what the author advocates." His query is answered in that "[t]he conventions of utopia provide that if the work contains a nonfictional section, its statements are to be taken as authoritative" (Morson 76). Of course, many editions of *Fahrenheit 451* contain nonfictional sections such as Bradbury's "Afterword" or "Coda." Here, like Bellamy's "Postscript" to *Looking Backward* (1986), Bradbury speaks for himself: "For it is a mad world and it will get madder if we allow the minorities, be they dwarf or giant, orangutan or dolphin, nuclear-head or water-conservationalist, pro-computerologist or Neo Luddite, simpleton or sage, to interfere with aesthetics" (178). Obviously, Bradbury's message is not in Montag or, as Touponce indicated, any single one-dimensional character. Bradbury's message is in the entire text and in the reader's response to it. In answer to the question "can books convert dystopia into utopia," Bradbury said "I feel that what I had to say in *Fahrenheit 451* is valid today and will continue to be valid here and in other countries in other years" (Spencer 2000, 104). He was right.

Works Cited

Amis, Kingsley. 2000. "A Skillfully Drawn Conformist Hell." *Readings on Fahrenheit 451*. Ed. Katie de Koster. San Diego, CA: Greenhaven Press, Inc., 93–99.

Bellamy, Edward. 1986. *Looking Backward*. New York: Penguin Books.

Bloom, Allan. 1968, "Interpretive Essay." *The Republic*. Translated by Allan Bloom. New York: Basic Books Inc., Publishers.

Bradbury, Ray. 1953. *Fahrenheit 451*. New York: Ballantine Books.

Hassler, Donald M. and Clyde Wilcox. 1997. "Introduction: Politics, Art, Collaboration." *Political Science Fiction*. Eds. Donald M. Hassler and Clyde Wilcox. Columbia, SC: University of South Carolina Press, 1–6.

Holtsmark, Erling B. 2001. "The Katabasis Theme in Modern Cinema." *Classical Myth & Culture in the Cinema*. Ed. Martin M. Winkler. New York: Oxford University Press.

Homer. 1996. *The Odyssey*. Translated by Robert Fagles. New York: Viking.

Homer. 1991. *The Iliad*. Translated by Robert Fagles. New York: Penguin Books.

Hoskinson, Kevin. 1995. "The *Martian Chronicles* and *Fahrenheit 451*: Ray Bradbury's Cold War Novels." *Extrapolation Vol* 36 #4 345–359.

Khanna, Lee Cullen. 1981. "The Reader and *Looking Backward*." *Journal of General Education* 33 (spring): 69–79.

Kirk, G. S. 1970. *Myth: Its Meaning and Functions in Ancient and Other Cultures*. Berkeley, CA: University of California Press.

McNelly, Willis E. 1982. "Ray Bradbury." *Science Fiction Writers: Critical Studies of the Major Authors from the Early Nineteenth Century to the Present Day*. Ed. E. F. Bleiler. New York: Charles Scribner's Sons, 171–178.

McNelly, Willis E. 1980. "Ray Bradbury—Past, Present, and Future." *Ray Bradbury*. Eds. Martin Harry Greenberg and Joseph D. Olander. New York: Taplinger Publishing Company, 17–24.

McGiveron, Rafeeq O. 1996. "What 'Carried the Trick'? Mass Exploitation and the Decline of Thought in Ray Bradbury's *Fahrenheit 451*." *Extrapolation Vol.* 37 #3, 245–256.

Mengeling, Marvin E. 1980. "The Machineries of Joy and Despair." *Ray Bradbury*. Eds. Martin Harry Greenberg and Joseph D. Olander. New York: Taplinger Publishing Company, 83–109.

Mogen, David. 1986. *Ray Bradbury*. Boston: Twayne Publishers.

Morson, Gary Saul. 1981. *Boundaries of Genre: Dostoevsky's Diary of a Writer and the Traditions of Literary Utopia*. Austin, TX: University of Texas Press.

Pell, Sarah-Warner J. 1980. "Style is the Man: Imagery in Bradbury's Fiction." *Ray Bradbury*. Eds. Martin Harry Greenberg and Joseph D. Olander. New York: Taplinger Publishing Company, 186–194.

Plato. 1968. *The Republic*. Translated by Allan Bloom. New York: Basic Books Inc., Publishers.

Plato. 1948. *The Portable Plato: Protagoras, Symposium, Phaedo, and The Republic*. Translated by Benjamin Jowett. New York: Viking Press.

Pohl, Frederick. 1997. "The Politics of Prophecy." *Political Science Fiction*. Eds. Donald M. Hassler and Clyde Wilcox. Columbia, SC: University of South Carolina Press, 7–17.

Reid, Robin Anne. 2000. *Ray Bradbury: A Critical Companion*. Westport, CT: Greenwood Press.

Sandoz, Ellis. 1971. *Political Apocalypse: A Study of Dostoevsky's Grand Inquisitor*. Baton Rouge, LA: Louisiana State University Press.

Sargent, Lyman T. 1975. "Utopia: The Problem of Definition." *Extrapolation* 16 (May): 137–48.

Seed, David. 1994. "The Flight from the Good Life: *Fahrenheit 451* in the Context of Postwar Dystopias." *Journal of American Studies* Vol. 28 #2, 225–240.

Sisario, Peter. 1970. "A Study of the Allusions in Bradbury's *Fahrenheit 451*." *English Journal* Vol 59, #2, 201–205, 212.

Spencer, Susan. 2000. "Can Books Convert Dystopia into Utopia?" *Readings on Fahrenheit 451*. Ed. Katie de Koster. San Diego, CA: Greenhaven Press, Inc., 100–106.

Spencer, Susan. 1999. "The Post-Apocalyptic Library: Oral and Literate Culture in *Fahrenheit 451* and *A Canticle for Leibowitz*." *Extrapolation* Vol 32 #4 331–142.

Strauss, Leo. 1959. *What is Political Philosophy? And Other Studies*. Glencoe, IL: The Free Press of Glencoe.

Strauss, Leo. 1964. *The City and Man*. Chicago: University of Chicago Press.

Touponce, William F. 1984. *Ray Bradbury and the Poetics of Reverie: Fantasy, Science Fiction, and the Reader*. Ann Arbor, MI: UMI Research Press.

Watt, Donald. 2000. "The Use of Fire as a Multifaceted Symbol." *Readings on Fahrenheit 451*. Ed. Katie de Koster. San Diego, CA: Greenhaven Press, Inc., 44–54.

Watt, Donald. 1980. "Burning Bright: *Fahrenheit 451* as Symbolic Dystopia." *Ray Bradbury*. Eds. Martin Harry Greenberg and Joseph D. Olander. New York: Taplinger Publishing Company, 195–213.

Wolfe, Gary K. 1980. "The Frontier Myth in Ray Bradbury." *Ray Bradbury*. Eds. Martin Harry Greenberg and Joseph D. Olander. New York: Taplinger Publishing Company, 33–54.

Zipes, Jack. 2000. "*Fahrenheit 451* Is a Reflection of 1950s America." *Readings on Fahrenheit 451*. Ed. Katie de Koster. San Diego, CA: Greenhaven Press, Inc. 124–133.

Zuckert, Catherine. 1990. *Natural Right and the American Imagination*. Savage, MD: Rowman & Littlefield Publishers, Inc.

JONATHAN R. ELLER AND
WILLIAM F. TOUPONCE

The Simulacrum of Carnival: Fahrenheit 451

THEMATICS

The main target of *Fahrenheit 451* is not censorship, as is often supposed, but rather mass culture, which Bradbury subjects to a Freudian critique like that given by Theodor W. Adorno and Max Horkheimer in *Dialectic of Enlightenment*.[26] *Fahrenheit* extrapolates into the future certain trends of the American cultural industry (*Kulturindustrie*—the term is Theodor W. Adorno's) observable during the 1950s, particularly the penetration of advertising and marketing techniques into every sphere of society. A central conviction of the book, as it was of "The Firemen," is that enlightenment and our increasingly rationalized civilization have produced not liberation, but further alienation.

The novel shows more clearly than the novella the antilife tendencies latent in what Adorno and Horkheimer call the enlightenment project, tendencies that can only culminate in the reduction of all higher values to a "paste pudding norm," as Captain Beatty, the defender of the status quo, succinctly puts it. Against this tendency toward "normalcy" and universalizing norms, Bradbury pits the protagonist, Montag, who wants to desire differently, not from lack and pseudoneeds created by the culture industry, but from plenitude of the will. The novel explores more fully than the novella the alternative possibilities of desiring things in a different way,

---

From *Ray Bradbury: The Life of Fiction*, pp. 186–207. © 2004 by the Kent State University Press.

suggesting to the reader through reveries of the material imagination an alternative to the values posited by mass culture. In effect, Montag's reveries of the earth help heal the split between man and nature, which rational enlightenment and science have brought about. The book ends by affirming the importance of the earth, which rises, phoenix-like, from the flames of mankind's self-destructive nihilism.

Thus, in its final and published form, *Fahrenheit 451* enacts a three-part diagnosis of the disease of modern man known as nihilism in its complete and incomplete varieties. The first part shows the hero becoming sick, the second deals with his rebellion and search for an antidote, and the third with a revaluation of values in which we learn the true worth of the principles put forth in the second part: the value of literacy, books, and reading in mass culture.

The medical terminology of sickness and health is consonant with Bradbury's own thematics in the novel. Indeed, there is a prominent thematic code in the book that organizes poisons and antidotes, infections and cures, and painkillers and stimulants, particularly with regard to the human bloodstream (as a metaphor for instinctive knowledge) and the stomach (as the capacity to digest or incorporate alien elements), which doubles as an indicator of moral strength, health, and sanity.

Once "infected" with the fever to read the books he normally burns, Montag the fireman is led on a search to find the origin of his unhappiness, and this leads him through certain stages of nihilism (discussed in detail below). However paradoxical it may sound at the outset of this discussion, what Montag discovers is that enlightenment must include a reversal of itself, that is, there should be a limit on enlightenment. He realizes that total science as an ideal leads to nihilism just as surely as Christian otherworldliness does. But any attempt to escape nihilism—understood here in the sense of the negation of the will to live—without reevaluating values simply produces the opposite, making the problem worse. Passing through pessimism, Montag at the end learns wisdom, what Nietzsche called the meaning of the earth, and thereby sets the limits of knowledge at what can be made instinctive, part of a bodily self, reflected symbolically in the bloodstream.

The philosophical position reached at the end, when Montag is living among a group of nomadic book-people, is best described as a determination to admit the necessity of constant revaluation to ourselves without any reservation, to stop telling ourselves tales in the old way. Hence the sense of pathos we feel in some of the speeches made by Granger, the spokesman of the itinerant book-people, a pathos that impels us to seek *new values* not necessarily defined, but nonetheless adumbrated by the novel itself. We learn that the world might be more valuable than once believed; we must see through the human tendency to make ideals fixed and eternal, for that is a denial of life and becoming. While we thought that we accorded the world the highest interpretation and value (the reader's experience in part 2, "The Sieve and the Sand"), we actually may not have given our existence even a moderately fair value.

To trace the itinerary of this revaluation and its stages is our task here. In the opening scene the landscape of this fantastic world is infested with a poisonous mythical monster, the salamander (metaphor for the fire engine) with its hose, described as a "great python spitting its venomous kerosene upon the world." We meet Montag, the agent of this poisoning, whose job it is to burn books that contain the memory of the past, the record of what different men and women have said and done throughout history. He destroys anything that might contradict the state's will to normalize and universalize truth, that is, that everything should be reduced to the thinkable in terms of mass norms. What remains is what Captain Beatty himself, in his own unwittingly ironic way, calls "noncombustible data," the facts of positivism that are supposed to make the people of this society feel brilliant without the need for interpretation.

At the outset, Montag is close to being a pyromaniac. He presides over a comic ritual that provides a carnival for the mass media to televise. Essentially, his nighttime job is entertainment in a society of spectacles, and he thoroughly identifies with it: the poisonous kerosene is perfume to him; a permanent fiery smile grips his face like a mask; and he winks at himself in the fire station mirror, his face burnt black, a minstrel man. When Montag meets his teenage neighbor, Clarisse, however, things begin to change. She has an impish sense of humor unknown to him (her "insanity," as she calls it) and little overt respect for the uniform he wears and its emblems of authority. Her constant wonder and curiosity, her intense *aliveness*, wakens Montag to a real world of sensations outside his ego's identification with its social role. Her function is to activate the dreaming pole of Montag's consciousness, long repressed by this technological society, and to stimulate reveries of the material imagination.

But her observations are also crucial to Montag's unmasking. She tells him, for example, that her education consists of "a lot of funnels and a lot of water poured down the spout and out the bottom, and them telling us it's wine when it's not"; wine is a symbol of health in this novel, as elsewhere in Bradbury. Clarisse diagnoses Montag with a dandelion flower, revealing to him that he really does not love anyone, that unhappiness is his true state of being. She runs off "across the lawn with the mask" that is his social persona, precipitating Montag's first reveries. She also tells him about a fireman who committed suicide by setting a mechanical hound against himself. Semiotically, the hound is one of the most overcoded bearers of the health–sickness distinction. It is an uncanny embodiment of the society's existential problems, which it has tried to banish by means of "healthful" technology, yet the "hounds" have come home, "full of poison wildness, of insanity and nightmare"; it murders its "sick" victims with a numbing dose of procaine. Because of her healthy family environment (which includes, according to her, being spanked when she needed it), Clarisse has been able to resist being shaped by the mass media. It is she who "infects" Montag with the desire to read the books he burns and the need to regain his psychic health.

Montag's wife, Mildred, is the thematic opposite of Clarisse. She embodies just about every form of self-narcotization available in this society and just about every way of avoiding the will to live and its affirmations. Deep down she is empty, suicidal, cruel. She attempts to hide this emptiness by various forms of artificial intoxication. Mildred keeps a miniature radio tamped in her ear at all times. She communicates with Montag by lip reading (training in such a skill having been thoughtfully supplied by the Sea Shell Company). She drives her car down the highways at tremendous rates of speed, hoping to kill an animal or, better yet, a human being. Mildred possesses a blind narcissistic enthusiasm for identifying with "exotic people's lives." Most of all she wants to buy another telescreen for their house, a fourth wall, to "make the dream complete." In appearance she is as thin as a praying mantis from dieting, her hair burnt to a brittle straw by dyeing, and her flesh described as the color of white bacon—not a healthy type to be sure. Mildred is a victim of mass culture and advertising that define desire as a lack and the consumer as someone whose desires can never be fulfilled. When Montag returns home after the book's opening conflagration and his encounter with Clarisse, he finds that his wife has attempted suicide by taking an overdose of sleeping pills. Later she is restored to "health" by an anti-suicide team and its machine, which fills her veins with the blood of a stranger. After this experience, Montag's faith in his marriage is profoundly shaken. He wonders whether he really knows this rosy-cheeked woman, or she him. He goes to sleep himself by taking a pill, saying that he does not know anything anymore.

This is the first stage of disorientation associated with nihilism. The second phase begins with Montag's growing alienation from his job, an alienation made complete after an incident in which an old woman chooses to die in the fire that destroys her house and hidden library rather than be taken to the insane asylum. While looting the ruins, Montag is seized with an uncontrollable desire to steal a book for himself after a falling volume accidentally lights in his hand, exposing its beautiful snowy pages painted with words. In this brief moment Montag is able to read one line of the book (which may possibly be a book of fairy tales). It is enough to convince him that there must be something in books that, once experienced, makes living life without them meaningless. He realizes that there is a person, an author behind every book.

As Nietzsche observed, the system of a philosopher may be dead and debunked, but the *person* behind it is incontrovertible; the person simply cannot be killed. The writer's literary force of personality continues to influence others, as Schopenhauer did Nietzsche. Books at this early stage of Montag's nihilism seem to represent a counterideal, offering a kind of transcendence. Metaphorically, books themselves are often compared to upwardly soaring birds, their pages to snowy feathers. They also seem to offer a new relationship to time—the kind of expansive and dreaming time associated with literary reverie. Soon after this incident, an intense physical need to read the books he has stolen overcomes Montag. Now he vomits at the smell of kerosene. A period of convalescence ensues during which the "fever" develops in terms of his search for new values: "So it was the hand that started it all. He felt one hand and then the other work his coat free and let it slump to the floor. He held his pants out into an abyss and let them fall into darkness. His hands had been infected, and soon it would be his arms. He could feel the poison working up his wrists and into his elbows and his shoulders, and then the jump over from shoulder blade to shoulder blade like a spark leaping a gap. His hands were ravenous. And his eyes were beginning to feel hunger, as if they must look at something, anything, everything."[27]

In his culture criticism, Nietzsche distinguishes neatly between one kind of cultural health that is defensive and restrictive and another that is marked by an abundant strength and vitality. Captain Beatty is an example of this former idea (and we will come to him presently), but this passage suggests the idea that Montag's illness will have a positive value and may even strengthen him. True, it exposes old illusions to an abyss, but it also bridges a gap between Montag and himself. Sickness is, then, actually good for him, a desirable challenge stimulating his powers. Montag now wants to see everything outside himself, is ravenously hungry for a world outside the self. Such a sickness, once overcome and incorporated, would leave him in a higher and enhanced state of health. Of course, in a sense this idea of well being collides with the romantic notion of perfect health embodied by Clarisse, for she is somehow untainted, untouched, and untroubled by any "fall" into sickness. She remains the inviolate utopian ideal of the novel, never burnt by the fireflies of any conflagration, and it seems that Bradbury, by having her die early in the novel, never seriously questions that ideal. Montag, however, has to cope with his disease (or "dis-ease," as Bradbury hyphenates it, making us read the word on the ontological level) brought on by her disappearance.

Before Montag can begin to read in earnest, however, Captain Beatty arrives to ask him when he will be well again. He gives Montag what he hopes will be an antidote for his sickness, which consists of a lesson in firemen history. Ironically, that account itself is an incisive indictment of the American culture industry. It describes the many forms of distorted communication taking place in the novel's society, from outright censorship of forbidden books to official state ideology with its leveling of all values to the unconscious and barbaric repetition of the same. Like a machine rotating on the same spot, Beatty's rhetoric gives us the impression of life and vitality, but it actually has none. It is a simulacrum of carnival, little more than a montage of superstructural effects that tells little about the basic economic conditions that led up to the present "utopia."

Beatty idolizes fire, the power of the state to reduce everything to ashy sameness and death. No minority differences are to be tolerated. Fire to him is precisely an antibiotic, an agent of stability and sanitation, for it seemingly destroys the upsurge of threatening new values. Although constantly changing and producing a fascinating world of phenomena, fire is an eternal value to him because it destroys differences. As an advocate of mass culture, he believes that everyone must be the same and desire the same things. Repetition of the same will, in turn, produces the greatest happiness for the greatest number of people. He understands Montag's attraction for books but claims that he himself overcame it. Yet significantly (and despite his apparent air of authority and even "beatitude"), he almost pleads with Montag not to allow "the torrent of melancholy and drear philosophy" to drown his happy world.

What Beatty fears most, we infer, is our present cultural situation with its conflict of interpretations. He only wants people to be crammed full of positivist facts that do not change, even though he ridicules the scientific explanation of fire in terms of friction and molecules as "gobbledygook." Facts are the important things to be desired, worn as emblems on every fireman's arm, like the fact that book paper catches fire and burns at 451 degrees Fahrenheit. His entire history is negative and defensive because he cannot affirm differences that are a result of the will to power playing itself out in events or in art. Beatty really is a nihilist. He argues that modern science has uncovered a bleak and useless existence that has made man feel only bestial and lonely. Beatty knows that man has lost dignity in his own eyes to an incredible extent in trying to equate the universe. And as for books, "Well, Montag, take my word for it, I've had to read a few in my time, to know what I was about, and the books say *nothing*! Nothing you can teach or believe. They're about nonexistent people, figments of imagination, if they're fiction. And if they're nonfiction, it's worse, one professor calling another an idiot, one philosopher screaming down another's gullet. All of them running about, putting out the stars and extinguishing the sun. You come away lost."[28]

Beatty is obsessed with the pessimistic "truth" about life but cannot see the value of literary fictions or their power as borrowed awareness. Why should we be concerned about the fate of a fictional character anyway? Beatty's philosophical position, which Nietzsche would surely have understood in all its implications as a form of nihilism, amounts to an absurd evaluation:

because of their pessimism, philosophers put out fires (stars and suns) instead of igniting them as the good optimistic firemen must do. Everyone needs the firemen to provide them with a show that takes away the burden of serious meaning.

Beatty's arguments defend a stage of nihilism Nietzsche calls "the last man."[29] To get an understanding of this stage, one must recall what Nietzsche says about the development of nihilism, which, by the way, he regards as the normal condition of man in culture, for he argues that it is in some fashion always present, *always* at work, before, during, and after the moment of its violent explosion.[30] But insofar as it is the peculiar disease of contemporary man (one requiring a homeopathic remedy), nihilism is also a passing pathological condition. At first, then, it is the disguised expression of a decadent will, of the impotent will to power recoiling from the affirmation of life and changing into negation. At this stage it may appear as the affirmation of grand supersensible values, the Platonic realm of ideas, which also supposedly possesses eternal being. In Nietzsche's view nihilism reactively creates a "true world" that possesses all the attributes life does not have: unity, stability, identity, and such, hence the division into two worlds, appearance and reality, that devalues life in favor of the otherworldly.

According to Nietzsche, as one goes through history, one finds the latent will for negation becoming more and more evident as more and more idols are smashed and replaced with new—and supposedly eternal—ones. The highest values constantly devaluate themselves, until humanity approaches the radical repudiation of all meaning, value, and desirability. Eventually, man comes to be so haunted by his own iconoclastic act that he cannot venerate himself, although he was powerful enough to kill God and to put science, or the modern technocratic state, in his place. This is roughly the stage Beatty claims to have passed through. Overtly, he confesses to no disgust with man anymore because he has found the true happiness of life in sameness, in mass culture. Paradoxically, the security of this happiness is derived from a perverse form of reading books that is also a fantastic reversal of enlightenment, in the sense that it idolizes fire and the way fire "consumes" meaning: "He could hear Beatty's voice. 'Sit down, Montag. Watch. Delicately, like the petals of a flower. Light the first page, light the second page. Each becomes a black butterfly. Beautiful, eh? Light the third page from the second and so on, chain smoking, chapter by chapter, all the silly things the words mean, all the false promises, all the second-hand notions and time-worn philosophies.' There sat Beatty, perspiring gently, the floor littered with swarms of black moths that had died in a single storm."[31]

How is this nihilistic happiness in reading to be understood? Certainly, chain smoking is a metaphor for the type of habituated mentality this society is seeking to produce in its consumers. Very little consciousness is required. What is more, here Beatty is doing it for spectacle, showing Montag the progressive consumption of everything having meaning, the growing predominance of empty significations, leading to the indefinite collapse and debacle of all meaning, all the "false promises" and "time-worn" philosophies of the past. The spiritual nihilism of the last man is ironically a product of the promise of the Enlightenment, here symbolized by man's technological control over fire.[32]

One possible interpretation here is that Beatty is parodying the determinate negation of significations that could be subsumed in a dialectical logic of enlightenment (such as that of Hegel). Instead of meaning being enriched by intellectual contradictions, Beatty's nihilistic reading transforms negations into unreadable black butterflies, which furthermore he finds beautiful. It is interesting to note that in the original typescript of the submitted novel, Bradbury had written "fantasies" after "false promises," which if left in would have served to make all the more clear Beatty's hostility to literary fantasy, which can represent a promise as broken (utopian longing can be evoked as unfulfilled). Beatty is one of those who teach contentment through the given norms of society, in this case supported by a cultural industry in which the firemen form a carnivalized sideshow.

The experience of true carnival, however, is not tainted with nihilism. Bradbury's thematics of fantasy in this utopian novel actually depends on the reader recognizing a distinction between two modes of fantasy: the spectacles of the mass media—the simulacrum of carnival—that promise satisfaction but in reality only serve to create anxiety about one's self-image by making an appeal to primitive narcissism, and literary reverie, which represents satisfaction and fulfillment not as a "false" promise, but as a "broken" promise, thereby putting the reader in a negative, or critical, position with regards to the former type of fantasy. The latter type represents true carnival because it creates new values and leads to a healthy (that is, not repressed) self. Clearly, Beatty does not want new values, only their repression. Like a moth fatally attracted to light, Beatty plays out all the dangers inherent in the Western program of enlightenment, which has tended to create a separation of our consciousness from nature through domination. But in the true body of carnival, man is a part of the natural world and the rhythms of life and death.

According to Nietzsche, this acute form of nihilism may abruptly alter its mood or tone, ceasing to be anxious inquietude, becoming instead a complacent quietude. Clearly, Beatty tries to convert Montag from the former to the latter by giving him a lesson in fireman history. He tries to sell his comrade on the idea of being a fireman again, to convert him back to the same. Thus, despite his idolization of fire—which would seem to present a world of changing and novel phenomena—his is really an appeal to sameness. We have in Beatty the experience of a will satisfied with meaninglessness, with nonsense, a will happy that there is no longer any meaning to seek, a will having found a certain comfort in the total absence of meaning and a happiness in the certainty that there is no answer to the question "What for?" He has become Nietzsche's "last man." Frozen at the stage of passive nihilism, rendered uniform, equal, and level, Beatty thinks he has invented happiness. But as Montag realizes in the climactic moment of the novel, *Beatty wants to die*. He deliberately provokes Montag into killing him with a flamethrower. Beatty's happiness is revealed as only apparently beatific. After the lecture, Montag allows that the captain is perhaps right—what is important is happiness. But this thought comes rather from the recognition that Montag himself is not, in fact, happy.

Bradbury constantly represents unhappiness in *Fahrenheit 451* as an emptiness that needs to be filled. Traditionally, beatitude has always been conceived of as a final state. It is always at the end of a certain "itinerary of the soul" that we find it as the fine flower consummating a great labor achieved. Yet happiness for Bradbury must come from affirmation and not negation, not as the end of a process oriented by some desired (and lost) object. Note that in the passage cited above, Beatty's nihilistic happiness-in-reading is also metaphorically a defloration of the text. The pages of the text are first petals that become black butterflies. That Bradbury wants to reject this idea of happiness along with Beatty is made evident in a scene in part 2 where the captain tells Montag of a dream of beatitude. His dream takes the form of a rhetorical battle of citations, with Montag trying to defend the integrity and ideal meaning of literature and Beatty taking the opposite tactic in quoting the books against themselves, displaying, in effect, his interpretive power over the text of this dream. By showing Montag that books can contradict themselves, Beatty apparently wins the battle and seems to stand on the side of reason. The dream ends with Montag climbing on board the salamander with Beatty and the both of them driving back to the firehouse "in beatific silence, all dwindled away to peace." In actuality, they drive off to burn Montag's own house, for Mildred has turned in the alarm on him.

Interestingly, when Bradbury read this novel for Harper Audio, he was careful to pronounce "Beatty" with three syllables so that it sounded like "beatitude." To Nietzsche, of course, an end to the freeplay of interpretation would be precisely an end to life: "There is no solely beatifying interpretation."[33] Although Bradbury may seem to side with Beatty in the sense that he too argues that texts need interpretation, in the end, he wants us to see Beatty's blissfulness as a manifestation of the death instinct, the silent instinct, the end to culture. In thus rejecting Beatty and his beatific readings of literature, we experience a major reversal of values, which prepares the way for a transformation of beatitude from a final to an initial state from which true happiness can then flow. We meet several of these states of being in part 3 of the novel, "Burning Bright."

These moments of plenitude and happiness are presented as "reveries of the material imagination" (the term is Gaston Bachelard's) when the human will spontaneously expresses itself in archetypal images—earth, air, fire, and water. Reverie is the primary means by which the reader, following Montag, explores the natural world and experiences imaginative forces that can create a human relationship to it. The absorption of the subject in fantasy into a material substance is experienced as a dynamic joy that participates in the life of that substance. Literary reverie becomes an act of consciousness by which the imagination overcomes alienation by *becoming* the world.

Before Bachelard's work on the material imagination, critics devoted little interest to Nietzsche's imagery, treating books such as *Thus Spoke Zarathustra* as primarily moral tracts. But Bachelard took Nietzsche's poetic images to be the very substance of his philosophical thought. For example, in his monograph on the German philosopher, Bachelard argues that the first transmutation of values experienced in *Zarathustra* is a transmutation of images. Reverie prepares the reader to experience the moral world of the text. Bachelard has no trouble in showing how and why Nietzsche devotes all his lyrical energy in the book to a change from heavy to light, from the terrestrial climate to the aerial. This creates for the reader a sense of overcoming the spirit of gravity, his primary antagonist. Cold, silence, and height are the components of what Bachelard calls Nietzsche's "oneiric temperament," the favorite region of the imagination in which he finds the image of his will. As he deftly says of the whole dialogic process, "Nietzsche gave the abyss the language of the summits" (*Il a fait parler aux abîmes le langage des sommets*).[34]

Similarly, in *Fahrenheit 451*, reveries of the will and material images are linked to the revaluation of values. They are active at all points in the text—especially in the fire imagery—at various levels of reader awareness. The imagery system of the novel has been a subject of interest among thematic critics, who have demonstrated the extensive use of images drawn from the elements of fire and water, though without linking them to values.[35] Mildred's *ressentiment*, for example, is a poisonous matter that accumulates like green stagnant water to which the eye of technology, as the embodiment of logical techniques, is blind. Fire is initially a force of negation that denies life and history. But in the third part of the novel, Montag experiences a series of reveries that reverse the values associated with these elements. In fact, it is by discovering how to dream well and in becoming master of his reveries that Montag satisfies that intense hunger for material images Clarisse had awakened in him, that is, those leading to a world outside the self. As he floats down a river away from the city, Montag learns to think about time in a reverie that restores his dynamic will to live, giving new values to fire and water. Later, he imagines himself taking on an animal's shape in the forest—thereby recovering his instinctive nature—and discovers a reverie of the forge that restores the power of language, so distorted in the city, to its proper capacity to reveal the meaning of things.

Here it is important to note that reverie is one of the ways in which Bradbury expanded "The Fireman" into a novel that itself brings neglected states of mind to light. Indeed, reverie plays no significant role in the novella, which is mainly concerned with a direct critique of mass culture. To present an alternative to mass culture, in later versions Bradbury greatly expanded the role of Clarisse as an agent of literary reverie. For instance, in the submitted manuscript of August 1953, Bradbury explicitly links the vision of the firelit camp (with the forge as the archetype structuring it) to Clarisse and to the conversations Montag heard while listening outside her house, especially "the rising falling voice of her uncle going on and on, comfortably, warmly, strangely, with wonder and fascination, in the late hours of the night." The entire paragraph makes clear the connection between reverie and the creative use of the powers of language. Although this was deleted in the finished novel, Montag still observes, just before he discovers the campfire, that Clarisse "had walked along here, where he was walking now."

One of the other striking omissions from the published version is a snow reverie that follows the destruction of the city. It is clear from the submitted manuscript that Bradbury originally intended the reveries of the earth that Montag experiences after emerging from the river to threaten to overwhelm him with sensations: "Where did you start? How did you keep your head above the surface of so much to learn? In a silence that was no silence, filled with a thousand wrigglings and shifting, crawlings, with burrowings and flakes of darkness touching at your face, moths, mosquitoes, flies, did you stop at your mouth and nose and eyes and die? Or did you stand, as he was now standing, and let it cover you until you were at the bottom of a stone well of odors and colors and shapes and blowing sounds?"

This passage presents an existential problem, which is also one of knowledge. Montag hungers for a healthful relationship with the earth, yet how can he manage the sensations that it brings? Two paths of struggle with these sensations, both equally fatal to the self, seem open. The first reverie is still based on water, keeping one's head above the surface and one's mouth and nose closed to sensations so that one eventually dies. The other is based on the archetype of the stone well, of water contained in the earth (remember that Montag has just emerged from water) and also leads to a kind of passivity and inundation. It is important to note the thematic paradoxes here: the earth is filled with threatening sensations leading to death and a "silence that was no silence." How does one silence this silence of the earth? How does one make it healthful, poetic, and meaningful?

Partly, this is accomplished by the reverie of the forge, which contains "a silence gathered all about that fire and the silence was in the men's faces, and time was there." This reverie of the forge (which Bachelard discussed as belonging to the thematics of the earth) is in both the novella and novel, but Bradbury no doubt felt the need for a stronger counter-reverie to nature's powers in the submitted manuscript. This took the form of an imagined snowfall, which becomes the very pattern of Montag's thought, truly silencing the earth:

> Montag watched the blood drip from his nose into the earth. He saw the pattern of his thoughts, stunned, shake down. Now it was the faintest blow of snowflakes on the first morning of great falling softness and silence when you squint to see the fine snow in the air and think it'll cover the ground. But it touches ground and vanishes as if eaten by the grass, but that's all right, there's more snow falling and falling, more tiny flecks fluttering down and you know that if you wait on it patiently there will be the first thin shell of rime and then a sugar-crust and then a thick frosting and then an abundance, enough thoughts and enough thinking in your head so you'll have enough clear drinking water as long as you wish, when ever you want to gather and melt it. The first snow was falling now, in his head.

Since the goal of this reverie is to get the earth and its plurality of meanings into the bloodstream in a healthful way, the passage begins with Montag dripping his own blood into the soil, beginning a kind of dynamic exchange and struggle with nature. This act of sacrifice generates the "pattern of his thoughts" that is equated with snowfall, which is thematically the anti-terrestrial matter Montag needs. Many poets whose imaginations have been attracted to snow have written about how it covers the ground with a whiteness and silence that truly overcomes its meanings, and reveries of snow in literature often manifest the spirit of negation, overturning, and conversion.[36] But Bradbury develops these literary and philosophical meanings in his own unique way. In his reverie the light snow is at first threatened by the grass, which might eat it, but as more falls the values are reversed until the snow becomes a delicious and life-sustaining food. Water is present in potential abundance; it can be eaten whenever Montag wants. Note too the phonetic prominence of the letter *f* alliterating throughout the passage—faintest, fluttering, falling, flecks—a snowfall of new meaning gathers itself in these words. This is more than just the use of a poetic technique. Matter and thought completely interpenetrate with language: "the first snow was falling now in his head." Bradbury's snowfall reverie equates the pattern of thought present in the image with the language of the text and with fullness of being, with plenitude and clear thought (drinking water).

But Bradbury removed the need for this imaginative counter-reverie when he toned down the threatening nature of the earth for the published version. A complete thematic reading of these passages is beyond the scope of this study. We can, however, give one brief example of language and reverie in the novel that will serve to show how the latter is tied thematically to moral and social codes as well as other texts in a poetic tradition.

American society as depicted in the novel has ceased to be sustained by any organized religion offering a center of meaning outside the self. Nothing replaces this loss of a center, but the mass media has set up grandiose narcissistic images of the self in the form of television media "families" who simulate happiness. Under these cultural circumstances Bradbury contrives to have his protagonist read out loud from the last two stanzas of Matthew Arnold's "Dover Beach," the most commented on poem in the English language. In Montag's society, this constitutes an open act of rebellion. He is asked by one of Mildred's uneasy guests whether or not the presence of the book indicates that he is reading up on "fireman theory." Montag responds by saying that it is not theory but poetry that the book represents.

The effect of this reading on Mildred and her friends, who are accustomed only to gratifying themselves obliviously with the latest "Clara Dove five-minute romance" on the wall-size television screens, is stunning. One woman sobs uncontrollably for her husband lost in the previous war, and another becomes enraged at being exposed to so much "poetry and sickness." Montag himself is overcome by the sudden appearance of authentic communication in the midst of the "empty desert," which is how Bradbury describes Montag's living room when the telescreens are turned off, and the idle chatter stops. It is important to understand here that Arnold's poem has come to signify, for us, the whole problem of modernity: in Nietzschean terms, how does one live meaningfully after the decline of religious beliefs (the death of God) and the demise of the Christian worldview that assigned humanity a clear place in creation? Science is no answer, for it too, as Captain Beatty indicates, only reveals a universe in which nature is indifferent to mankind's purposes.

Is literature then an answer? Is Bradbury appropriating Arnold's poem nostalgically, yearning after a lost center of culture, longing for some ideal of communication whose origins lie in the past? Yes, but only partially. Bradbury is also showing us the real value of "Dover Beach" for our age of mass communications Arnold subscribed to a liberal ideal of radiant literacy. He conceived of culture as a pursuit of our total perfection based, in part, on our getting to know the best that has been thought and spoken in the past (his famous "touchstones"). Furthermore, for Arnold, culture meant criticism, especially when these touchstones are applied to the present; without it, man remains a creature limited by self-satisfaction. This ideal of culture and criticism is surely Bradbury's own in the novel, for he makes Arnold's poem resonate in new ways. Unlike the debased romanticism of Clara Dove, Arnold's poem definitely does not have a happy ending and therefore no overt appeal to narcissism (though the reverie of the Sea of Faith evokes melancholy to be sure). The speaker of Arnold's poem is trying to enunciate to his beloved how he authentically feels about the state of the world and the possibilities for communication in it, the world that seems to lie before them like a land of dreams but that really has neither joy, nor love, nor peace in it. He has to emerge from darkness to see the landscape that lies about him and to see himself in that landscape.

The poem becomes an instance of the authentic use of language to communicate emotions between people. "Fireman theory" will not be capable of explaining away the powerful feelings it evokes. One of the most influential modern theories of literature, Russian formalism, argues that art and its techniques are designed to slow down perception and make us perceive again with a fresh vision what has become worn out and stale, second nature. By building such an interpretive frame around the reading of Arnold's poem, Bradbury, in essence, tells us that as long as humanity remembers one poem from the best of our literature, the effects of habituation, which threaten like fire to devour families, friends, and even fear of war, will find it more difficult to settle in. In particular, the last line of Arnold's poem about ignorant armies clashing by night is "defamiliarized" and rings true in a new way for this society, which has fought and quickly forgotten three atomic wars in the recent past.

The simulacrum of carnival—including three-dimensional "sex magazines"—has almost completely supplanted "authentic" and difficult philosophical meanings evoked by literature such as "Dover Beach." Beatty's earlier comment to Montag that "pleasure lies all about after work" in forms of mass entertainment is probably an ironic echo of the famous line in Arnold's poem about the world lying before the lovers "like a land of dreams." This cultural situation of absolute vulgarity and violence is something Bradbury seems to have been thinking about early in his career and well before the publication of "The Fireman." Among his unpublished novel projects dating from 1947 is *Where Ignorant Armies Clash by Night*, which depicts a situation of near absolute nihilism and vulgarity (in the planned last chapter, published in 1952 as "The Smile," people line up to spit on the Mona Lisa). The story is set in a barren postapocalyptic United States two centuries in the future, in which cultural values have been profoundly inverted. Society is held together by ritualized Roman circus-like ceremonies in which people are murdered by the Assassins, or Great Killers, a guild of honored warrior-killers who also—and this is its thematic link with *Fahrenheit 451*—burn and mutilate books for the adoring crowds. The last copy of the Bible is scheduled to be destroyed during an upcoming carnival in New Orleans. Books have become the center and focus of the democratic crowd's hatred for "elite" culture (such as Shakespeare). The plot in one version has the assassin Muerte—like Montag—begin reading the books he is destroying. This reading in turn provokes a profound crisis of values in which the hero revolts against the democratic masses, discovering "the violence of writing" as he tries to make a copy of the last Shakespeare text before it is destroyed. His story does not end happily. Because of these actions, he becomes one of society's outcasts, not touchable or killable. Finally, a committee of elders comes to him offering death by suicide (poison), considered a highly dishonorable death, and Muerte accepts. Before he dies, he makes a speech in which he identifies with the authors he knows, "I am Byron, I am Shakespeare, I am Poe, I am Plato, . . ." expressing the idea that when he dies, they too will die. Interestingly, Muerte has heard stories of "people *who* are the books" living somewhere in the world and thinks of organizing them together into one community.

Of course, *Fahrenheit 451* is set at a stage of future nihilism long past that which troubled Arnold, who does lament the loss of a transcendental center (that is, God) that would give meaning to the world, but nevertheless, the poem is not being used nostalgically. Rather, it is being made to serve the function of awakening people to the fact that there is no eternal world of happiness, that one cannot escape the inevitable pain and suffering of life, despite what the illusions of the culture industry may say. Bradbury's reading of Arnold may also suggest here a kind of critique of critique, telling us that the use of tradition is to remind the critique of ideology that humanity can project its emancipation into the future and anticipate an unconstrained and unlimited communication only on the basis of the creative reinterpretation of the cultural heritage. If we had no experience of authentic communication, however restricted and mutilated it was, how could we ever wish it to prevail for all people? He who is unable to reinterpret his past may also be incapable of projecting concretely his interest in emancipation.

Compare *Fahrenheit 451* to *Where Ignorant Armies Clash by Night* with regards to the stages of nihilism. The entire text of Arnold's "Dover Beach" is cited in the unpublished novel because, in that story, his writings have, ironically, become so little known. As in *Fahrenheit*, at the heart of *Ignorant Armies* lies a struggle with the modern crisis of values, with nihilism, which is explained in a speech by the "old man" (unnamed in the manuscript) to the child he is educating. His words show that he is a clear analogue to "wise old man" figures in the utopian-dystopian genre (and to Nietzsche's soothsayer figure in part 2 of *Thus Spoke Zarathustra*): "Everything is futile, all effort is in the end worthless. A man may, of course, still pursue disconnected ends, money, fame, art, science, and may gain pleasure from them. But life is hollow at the center. Hence the dissatisfied, disillusioned, restless, spirit of modern man. Hence Death as a value. If Life has no Value, then give Death a value." It is clear that Muerte (Death) the assassin is an almost allegorical figure, and the perverted carnival over which he presides is an attempt to "make a religion of Meaninglessness." But the perverted carnival can never create new values, not even when it is later supported by the efforts of the full-blown mass media depicted in *Fahrenheit 451*. It remains a performance for spectators, though it is considered an honor to die in such a spectacle.

The wise old man sees no way out of nihilism, which goes in cycles, but thinks that this new religion of Death can at least offer certainty if not hope: "Let man for the first time revoke the natural laws of survival and self-preservation. Self-preservation? For what, for purposes of life? No, no! Man now wades further and further out into the black deep tarpit of Death. Soon he will slide from view. Then the animals will come. The whole thing will start again, from Faith to Faithlessness, from Meaning to Meaninglessness.... And this man, this great William Donne [Muerte], is our god, and we his disciples, revolting against meaninglessness, dying proud and true to our values, cynical as they may seem." This "god," however, is himself infected with a weariness of spirit toward "the wonderfully negative world of killing and being killed" that would have confounded Nietzsche. Muerte sees everyone, including himself, as ignorant and stupid fools "rolling in the filth" of human degradation and desperately wants to smash the system of false entertainments, of "banquets, feasts, and festivals," over which he presides. He remains powerless to do so, however.

Bradbury had plans to introduce another character, William Elliott, who may have been an assassin himself and took to reading books to the crowd. It is he who reads "Dover Beach" to the people before giving it to them, burning it leaf by leaf, "as if hands of fire were turning each page, scanning and burning with the same fire," in a scene whose language looks forward to that of Beatty's nihilistic reading. But in *Ignorant Armies*, the burning pages are caught by the crowd "in eager hands and clenched and popped into mouths like sweetmeats," which suggests a cannibalistic feast. Elliott would subvert the system by pleading with Muerte to spare his life, and indeed he is given a long speech in part of a stage version of the manuscript that Bradbury was working on simultaneously. In this he calls himself "a flame in the wilderness" that can "burn you clean of your oppression and night melancholy" with the good knowledge that "we live and therefore our [*sic*, probably "are"] blessed." But Muerte is unable to affirm his life, to accept the blessing, which is developed in *Fahrenheit 451* as the meaning of the earth, and slays Elliott.

Montag only learns this power of affirmative utopian values through the experience of reading and reverie, which becomes foregrounded in the second part of the novel in such scenes as where Montag's hunger cannot be satisfied by the spectacles of the mass media. Indeed, his society seems to have lost the knowledge of the real feeling of satisfaction or happiness. Another scene, set in a subway, has Montag trying to read from the Bible Jesus' parable of the lilies of the field (in the text of Matthew's gospel) to memorize and understand its import while loudspeakers are blaring out a mindless commercial about dental hygiene. It is only when Montag reaches Faber, an old, retired English teacher, that he receives something like an antidote to his "dis-ease." Faber is a sort of failed Northrop Frye, for he knows that the secular scripture represented by books did nothing to stop the onset of barbarism, but nonetheless he affirms that the media could be used to accommodate Arnold's ideal of radiant literacy. This ideal has not been disproved, even if it has failed to materialize, he seems to say.

Faber tells Montag that he is a "hopeless romantic" for believing that books themselves are what he needs, though Faber does not deny that there are authentic *persons* behind them. He tells Montag that books are hated and feared because they show the pores in the face of life. Furthermore, on close inspection by the intellect, they reveal themselves precisely as texts, which "stitch the patches of the universe together into one garment for us." That is their only magic. And at least they cannot entirely delude readers into believing that they are all of one piece, without gaps, at the origin. The study of literature begins precisely with textual criticism—these "patches" of other texts—and with intertextuality, such as the way in which Bradbury himself appropriates and renews the meaning of Arnold's poem. In books, which can always be shown to be texts, the human will to truth cannot become total. We are allowed the play of interpretation. This is quite unlike the spectacle of the mass media, where the environment is as real as the world: "It *becomes* and is the truth." Nonetheless, and despite these indications of critical reading Faber wants to inculcate in Montag, he first tries to awaken in him a nostalgia for the meaning of the earth. In oneiric terms, Faber introduces him to reveries of the earth and the will by telling him a myth:

> We are living in a time when flowers are trying to live on flowers, instead of growing on good rain and black loam. Even fireworks, for all their prettiness, come from the chemistry of the earth. Yet somehow we think we can grow, feeding on flowers and fireworks, without completing the cycle back to reality. Do you know the legend of Hercules and Antaeus, the giant wrestler, whose strength was incredible so long as he stood firmly on the earth? But when he was held, rootless, in midair, by Hercules, he perished easily. If there isn't something in that legend for us today, in this city, in our time, I am completely insane.[37]

Faber arranges to communicate more of this earthly wisdom by implanting an electronic device in Montag's ear and reading to him from the Bible (exclusively from the Book of Job in "The Fireman," but from Ecclesiastes and Revelations primarily in the finished novel). Listening to the "delicate filigree" of the old man's voice in the following days and nights, Montag's imagination produces its own antidote to the poisons of mass culture through a reverie of the earth." He imagines that fire and water, Montag plus Faber, will combine to form a new substance, a new self, symbolized by wine. Wine is one of Bradbury's major symbols of life, and it is thematically appropriate here because it comes from the soil and "remembers" the climate that produces it. Furthermore, it has long been considered a health-giving liquid that, once in the body, warms and refreshes because it has qualities of both fire and water. It is in itself a living body that balances the heavy and the light, a conjunction of earth and sky, an image of health.

Montag's reverie, which seems to progress in a dialectical fashion, is really an interpretation. He needs this notion to believe in his own value again. Faber destroys Montag's romantic illusions but nonetheless rescues him from total nihilism by providing him with a myth to awaken his dreaming capacity. It fosters in Montag the desire for a kind of instinctive knowledge of the body, though certainly not a longing for another world. These values are, in turn, revalued at the end of part 3.

There are a series of reveries leading up to this revaluation and reversal that come after Montag sets aflame his own house in a conflagration that also kills Beatty, destroys a mechanical hound, and then escapes from the city. The most important of the series for present purposes is the long water reverie. In it, Montag learns to "will backwards," to affirm the passage of time and to liberate himself from the entire weight of the negative. Floating peacefully on his back in a river, looking at the reflected light of the moon, Montag realizes that all knowledge is "solar," that is, active interpretation. As Nietzsche would say, there is no immaculate perception.[38] Montag realizes through reverie that he cannot, like the Moon, simply reflect in contemplation his love of the earth. It must be willed:

> The sun burnt every day. It burnt Time. The world rushed in a circle and turned on its axis and time was busy burning the years and the people anyway, without any help from him. So if *he* burnt things with the firemen and the sun burnt Time, that meant *everything* burnt!
>
> One of them had to stop burning. The sun wouldn't, certainly. So it looked as if it had to be Montag and the people he had worked with until a few short hours ago.[39]

The realization that things go in cycles of nihilism, without the ego consciously willing it, could crush Montag at this point if he were not protected by the water of his reverie. Here again we have the image of nihilism as a fire that inexhaustibly and voraciously appropriates everything strange or new in life with a view to reducing it to sameness. If allowed to progress to the limit, it would reduce all values to falsity (the essence of Beatty's reading of texts). To overcome himself, Montag the fireman vows never to burn again. This is an affirmation, not a negation—one that furthermore affirms everything against which Beatty directed his destructive dialectic. It is the emergence of differences and the will affirming and interpreting itself in time. Montag realizes not only that the world is full of burning of all types and sizes but also that "the guild of the asbestos weaver must open shop very soon," weaving texts that once again will sustain humanity. It is only thus that the becoming of the world can be redeemed, and Montag goes on to dream forward about Clarisse in a vision of the utopian ideal, never burnt by the fireflies of any conflagration. After this reverie, in which he interprets his life backward and forward in time, he emerges from the river a happy man, discovering delight in the miraculous presence of natural objects liberated from the oblivion in which technological thinking casts them.

By bringing Clarisse down to earth onto an idealized image of a farm he remembers from his childhood, Montag has learned the meaning of nature and no longer needs any outside authority to give his life meaning, whether it be the state or books themselves. He goes on to walk through a forest in which he imagines himself an animal, "a thing of brush and liquid eye," until he finds the campfire of the book people, where a collective reverie of the forge is in progress. It is perhaps the strongest image of the human will in the novel. As such, it completely reverses the values previously associated with fire, now becoming humanly warming, and it places time at the service of the men whose voices have the power to talk about everything (that is, language is no longer used for the purposes of domination) as they "look at the world and turn it over with the eyes, as if it were held to the center of the bonfire, a piece of steel these men were shaping."

Among them, Montag is given a new "identity" (if we can call becoming a text anything like becoming self-identical). There is even a joke about not judging a book by its cover, for some of their members have had plastic surgery to disguise themselves. Montag, who has believed that there is a person behind every book, is now self-consciously and playfully becoming a mask. This indicates among other things that he can no longer take his fireman persona—at least insofar as it had been imposed on him by the simulacrum of carnival—so seriously. In fact, Montag is directly told that only the book he has memorized (with the help of Faber) is really important. In the society of the book people, there is a resistance to narcissism.

The social organization of these people is nomadic and antidialectical in structure, described as flexible, very loose, and fragmentary (some people are only chapters of books, as is Montag). The book people are not reconciled to each other in any totalizing vision but rather affirm a radical pluralism. Each man's memorization of a text he loves is the willful and selective affirmation of a self or mask in its positive difference from other masks. They represent a nomadic flow of desire outside the territorial codings of the state into what Bradbury refers to as a "wilderness."

Most Bradbury critics confine their study of the wilderness myth in his writings to *The Martian Chronicles*, but it is clearly operative here as well. Only the myth of the wilderness and its nomads are able to withstand the apocalyptic force of destruction that is finally unleashed in an atomic war, destroying the major cities. It is after this final outbreak of destructive nihilism, however, that Montag learns that man has not valued the earth enough: "Look at the world out there ... outside me, there beyond my face and the only way to really touch it is to put it where it's finally me, where it's in the blood, where it pumps around a thousand times ten thousand a day."[40]

It would seem that Montag must renew his vow to remain faithful to nature, to give the earth a human meaning. The problem of getting this into the blood was originally taken care of by the snow reverie, which starts with sacrificial blood dripping from Montag's nose into the soil and which follows immediately on the passage cited above. Because of the presence of such strong reveries, even after a nuclear war, man and man's earth appear to him as inexhaustible and still undiscovered. Bradbury's diagnosis of modern culture ends with the emergence of a healthy body that can manifest the meaning of the world.[41] Yet there is hardly an overt myth of the overman (who in Nietzsche's philosophy is the meaning of the earth) in this novel as there was at the end of *The Martian Chronicles*, unless Montag, with his hopeful healing vision of the future, is a presage of one, of a being who is cured of the "sickness of man." The book people themselves are not at all sure that they can "make every future dawn glow with a purer light," and they certainly do not imagine that becoming books affords them any security. Perhaps they correspond to a stage of incomplete nihilism that Nietzsche called "the higher man," those who are the last vestiges of God on earth, in the sense that they desperately uphold an ideal of radiant literacy, the fragility of which they know all too well.[42] After all, even when men possessed books, it did not stop them from destroying themselves, as Faber points out to Montag.

Granger's angry and abusive speech about man being a first cousin to the phoenix, a "silly damn bird" whose origins are "back before Christ," brings the theme of fire back into the text. It is important to understand how this theme of fire is related both to true and inverted carnival. In many respects fire in carnival is an expression of what Bakhtin calls "the ancient ambivalence of the death wish, which also sounds like a wish for renewal and rebirth: die, and live again."[43] Carnival was always utopian for Bakhtin, its fires symbolically destroying the rigidified past and opening onto a new and less terrifying future, more related to the life of the earth and the body. Here, at the end of *Fahrenheit 451*, fire is an agent not only of destruction again but also of renewal, for the phoenix gets himself "born all over again." Clearly, this is different from Beatty's nihilistic use of fire, which destroys all values; his use could never be affirmed and lead to rebirth. And the fact that frank language has been liberated here too (ironically, the expletives, four "damns" and one "goddamn," would be censored in the Bal-Hi version of *Fahrenheit 451*, eliminating much of the emotional effect of this passage and others as well) indicates that Montag is in the presence of a new order of society in which there is no fear of using unofficial language. In addition to the abuse heaped on man—his silly tendency to build funeral pyres and to leap onto them—there is also praise—man remembers "all the damn silly things" he has done in the past and can overcome them if he so desires. Humans are not simply subject to animal drives, like the phoenix, and maybe some day the destructive aspects of carnival will no longer be necessary.

There is a definite suggestion in Granger's speech about the phoenix that cultural nihilism tends to run in cycles (this is also evident in the wise old man's speech to the child in *Where Ignorant Armies Clash by Night*). Is knowing and affirming this "wisdom" of any value? Bradbury seems to suggest that it is without asking us to embrace fully the dread Nietzschean notion of eternal return. That, we take it, is the point of the quotations from chapter 3 of Ecclesiastes. This wisdom book of the Bible is famous, of course, for the assertion that "there is nothing new under the sun" and for the view that there is a time for every purpose under heaven. While some have labeled its author a pessimist weary of life, we think rather that the wisdom of the intertext here is that only when men are aware that nothing is really new can they live with an intensity in which everything can potentially become new. The spectacles of mass culture that Montag has escaped are based on the false illusion of continual newness. Some "disillusionment" is therefore necessary first in order to experience what newness of life truly is. Then we are prepared to understand the value of the tree of life, an image from both the beginning—the garden of Eden—and the end—the Revelation of the New Jerusalem—of the Bible. For Bradbury, the tree of life's real cultural nourishment lies in the ability of mankind's imaginative vision (with twelve kinds of fruit yielded every month—it is an abundant tree) to sustain us in affirming the value and meaning of life in this world.

In this manner *Fahrenheit 451* posits a utopian ideal of ironic enlightenment among the damaged lives of its cultural outsiders ("hobo intellectuals" as they are called in "The Fireman"—they only remember bits and pieces of texts, not whole books), who embrace the ambivalent contradictions of life and textuality and who would not want to abolish them in the name of conformity to social norms, a major preoccupation of the status quo in the

1950s (Beatty tells Montag that society functions best when all are the same). *Fahrenheit* is a book that connects its readers with some of culture's great literary voices, the value of that conversation becoming apparent through the book's critique of mass culture. Indeed, in the novel's last few sentences, Montag is presented as a man who has mastered a great inner emptiness of nihilism and who now feels not emptiness, but a kind of instinctive memory, the "slow stir of words, the slow simmer," that is associated with literary reverie. The promise given by the ending of the novel is that Montag will now speak freely and create values from an initial happiness and plenitude, from a sense of a new beginning, which also revalues the utopian tradition. Quoting from the "defamiliarized" Bible, three times reiterating the word "yes," what could be more appropriate than that Montag, who now embodies the meaning of the Earth, should quote the words of the preacher in Ecclesiastes about the seasons and the words from the Apocalypse of Saint John, one text declaiming all the vanities of this world and the other asserting the need for a new world in the lines about the tree of life, rooted now in *this* world, whose leaves are for the healing of nations? The reader feels assured that these words will be spoken when Montag reaches the earthly city and not the heavenly one.

The most significant thematic development between the text of "The Fireman" and *Fahrenheit 451* was the series of reveries based on the material imagination (earth, air, fire, water) that guide Montag's—and the reader's—growing realization of the meaning of the world in the expanded novel text. In his next book, Bradbury structured an entire novel with reveries that combine these traditional four elements together, his master metaphor *Dandelion Wine*.

NOTES

26. Theodor W. Adorno and Max Horkheimer, "The Culture Industry: Enlightenment as Mass Deception," in *Dialectic of Enlightenment*, trans. John Cumming (New York: Seabury, 1972), 120–67. Adorno and Horkheimer are concerned in their analyses with the notion of domination, which not only affects society but also extends to nature. They argue that this was one of the results of the Enlightenment and has become nearly total in our modern technological civilization. According to them, Nietzsche saw both aspects of the Enlightenment, "both the universal movement of sovereign Spirit (whose executor he felt himself to be), and a 'nihilistic' anti-life force in the enlightenment." Ibid., 44. We are indebted to their discussions in our understanding of Bradbury's development of these ideas. They too link the culture industry to a simulacrum of carnival (ibid., 143) and see laugher as perverted by it: "In the false society laughter is a disease which has attacked happiness and is drawing it into its worthless totality." Ibid., 141. They help us understand how Bradbury can be at the same time critical of myths created by modern mass culture and a writer of myths himself. His myths in *F451*, such as the myth of the wilderness and the myth of Antaeus, are not about domination and exploitation, but about the need to rediscover the meaning of the earth, which lies outside of any notion of progress.

27. *F451*, pt. 1, 41.

28. Ibid, 62.

29. See Nietzsche, "Zarathustra's Prologue," *Thus Spoke Zarathustra*, in *Portable Nietzsche*, 129–30.

30. The various stages of nihilism are presented in Nietzsche, *Will to Power*, bk. 1, 7–82. They are schematized by Michel Haar, "Nietzsche and Metaphysical Language," in *The New Nietzsche: Contemporary Styles of Interpretation*, ed. David B. Allison (New York: Delta, 1977), 12–16. Our discussion here is indebted to Haar's schematization, but Nietzsche too describes nihilism as a psychological state of exhaustion in which the soul, which longs to admire and revere, finds itself wallowing in "the idea of some supreme from of domination and administration." Nietzsche, *Will to Power*, bk. 1, 12. This, in part, explains Beatty's worshipful attitude toward fire, in which he rejects what science reveals about it—he knows full well that science and reason cannot create values. Of course, his fascination with fire does not create life-affirming values for him but rather destroys them.

31. *F451*, pt. 2, 76–77.

32. "Enlightened by Hobbes and Locke to the fear of death as the fundamental fear, Zarathustra's audience [the last man] is in the process of surrendering all aspiration except for comfortable self preservation." Lampert, *Nietzsche's Teaching*, 25. Lampert's discussion of the figure of the last man in Nietzsche's text has guided our own discussion here. He points out that the last men are those "of technological mastery" among whom uniformity and sameness have prevailed. But although the last men have won out in the struggle against the forces of inequality and scarcity in nature, their happiness is fragile, for it requires recognition and reassurance from others like themselves. Most devastating is the global effect of their reign, for the universal domination of the last men prevents the Earth from having any meaning. We have taken Beatty to be one of the last men, a representative of that final and most dangerous form of nihilism (per Lampert) brought about, in Nietzsche's view, by universal claims of the democratic enlightenment that abolishes all differences or diverts them into the madhouse (what the authorities intend to do with people like Clarisse, whose name ironically means light and illumination). Beatty celebrates the pleasures of the last man, which Nietzsche mocked as "wretched contentment," and derides any attempt to pursue higher spiritual values as doomed to failure from the outset.

33. Nietzsche to Carl Fuchs, Aug. 26, 1888, as quoted in Michael Haar, "Nietzsche and Metaphysical Language," in *The New Nietzsche*, ed. David B. Allison (New York: Dell, 1977), 7.

34. Gaston Bachelard, *L'Air et les songes* (Paris: Corti, 1943), 146–85. Bachelard, in fact, wrote two studies of reveries of the earth, which serves to indicate the importance of this element to the poetic imagination. The forge, which Montag discovers in the third part of the book, is discussed by Bachelard as one of the reveries of the will. In his other book Bachelard studies the earth in relation to reveries of rest and repose, which also can be found in this section of the book when Montag enters the hay barn. Selections from his writings about literary reveries of the material imagination can be found in *On Poetic Imagination and Reverie*, trans. with an introduction by Colette Gaudin (New York: Bobbs-Merrill, 1971). These studies broaden and deepen our understanding of the meaning of the Earth in *Fahrenheit 451*.

35. Donald Watt, "Burning Bright: *Fahrenheit 451* as Symbolic Dystopia," in Olander and Greenberg, *Ray Bradbury*, 195–213.

36. Gilbert Durand, "Psychanalyse de la neige," *Mercure de France* 1, no. 8 (1953): 615–39.

37. *F451*, pt. 2, 83.

38. See "On Redemption," pt. 2 of *Thus Spoke Zarathustra*, in *Portable Nietzsche*. For willing backward, see "On Immaculate Perception," in ibid.

39. *F451*, pt. 3,141.

40. Ibid., pt. 3,162.

41. See Nietzsche, "On the Afterworldly," pt. 1 of *Thus Spoke Zarathustra*, in *Portable Nietzsche*.

42. Nietzsche, "On the Higher Man," pt. 4 ibid.

43. Bakhtin, *Rabelais*, 249.

Chronology

1920	Born August 22 in Waukegan, Illinois, the third son of Leonard Spaulding Bradbury, an electrical lineman, and Esther Marie Moberg Bradbury, a native-born Swede. His twin brothers had been born in 1916; one died in 1918.
1926	Sister Elizabeth is born; family moves to Tucson, Arizona, in the fall.
1927	Elizabeth dies of pneumonia; family returns to Waukegan in May.
1932	Father laid off from job as telephone lineman; family moves back to Tucson.
1933	Family moves back to Waukegan.
1934	Seeking employment, father moves family to Los Angeles.
1938	Graduates from Los Angeles High School; first short story, "Hollerbochen's Dilemma," published in *Imagination!*
1939	Sells newspapers on Los Angeles street corner.
1942	Begins earning $20 a week writing short stories and decides to quit selling newspapers to write full time.
1947	Marries Marguerite McClure. Publishes *Dark Carnival.*
1949	First daughter born.
1950	*The Martian Chronicles* published.
1951	*The Illustrated Man* published. Second daughter born.
1953	*The Golden Apples of the Sun* and *Fahrenheit 451* published.

1955	*Switch on the Night*, a children's book, published. *The October Country* published. Third daughter born.
1957	*Dandelion Wine* published.
1958	Fourth daughter born.
1959	*A Medicine for Melancholy* published.
1962	*Something Wicked This Way Comes* and *R Is for Rocket* are published.
1963	Publishes first collection of drama, *The Anthem Sprinters and Other Antics*.
1964	*The Machineries of Joy: Short Stories* published. *American Journey*, his film history of the nation opens at the New York world's fair; produces *The World of Ray Bradbury* at the Coronet Theatre, Los Angeles.
1965	*The Vintage Bradbury* published.
1966	Francois Truffaut's movie *Fahrenheit 451* released. *Twice Twenty-Two*, *Tomorrow Midnight*, and *S Is For Space* are published.
1969	Film version of *The Illustrated Man* released. *I Sing the Body Electric!* published.
1972	*The Wonderful Ice Cream Suit and Other Plays* and *The Halloween Tree* published.
1973	*When Elephants Last in the Dooryard Bloomed*, Bradbury's first collection of poetry, published.
1975	*Pillar of Fire and Other Plays* published.
1976	*Long after Midnight* published.
1977	*Where Robot Mice and Robot Men Run Round in Robot Towns*, a collection of poetry, published.
1979	*This Attic Where the Meadow Greens* published.
1980	*The Stories of Ray Bradbury* and *The Last Circus* and *The Electrocution* published.
1981	*The Haunted Computer and the Android Pope*, a collection of poetry, published.
1982	*The Complete Poems of Ray Bradbury* and *The Love Affair* published.
1983	*Dinosaur Tales* published.
1984	Film version of *Something Wicked This Way Comes*, from a screenplay by Bradbury, released. Collection of early mystery stories, *A Memory of Murder*, published.

1987	*Death Has Lost Its Charm for Me* and *Fever Dream* published.
1988	*The Toynbee Convector*, a collection of stories, published.
1989	*The Climate of Palettes* published.
1990	*The Day It Rained Forever*, a musical, published; also publishes two novels, *A Graveyard for Lunatics* and *Another Tale of Two Cities*.
1991	*Yestermorrow: Obvious Answers to Impossible Futures*, a book of essays, published.
1992	*Green Shadows, White Whale*, a novel, published.
1996	*Quicker Than the Eye*, a collection of stories, published.
1997	*Driving Blind*, a collection of stories, published. Also published *With Cat for Comforter* and *Dogs Think That Every Day Is Christmas*.
1998	*Ahmed and the Oblivion Machines* published.
2001	*A Chapbook for Burnt-out Priests, Rabbis and Ministers* and *From the Dust Returned* published.
2002	*One More for the Road* published.
2003	*Bradbury Stories* published. Wife dies.
2003	*Let's All Kill Constance* published.
2004	Awarded the National Medal of Arts by President George W. Bush and First Lady Laura Bush. *The Cat's Pajamas* published.
2005	*Bradbury Speaks* published.
2006	*The Homecoming* and *Farewell Summer* published.
2007	*Now and Forever* published. Receives special citation from the Pulitzer Board.

Contributors

HAROLD BLOOM is Sterling Professor of the Humanities at Yale University. He is the author of 30 books, including *Shelley's Mythmaking*, *The Visionary Company*, *Blake's Apocalypse*, *Yeats*, *A Map of Misreading*, *Kabbalah and Criticism*, *Agon: Toward a Theory of Revisionism*, *The American Religion*, *The Western Canon*, and *Omens of Millennium: The Gnosis of Angels, Dreams, and Resurrection*. *The Anxiety of Influence* sets forth Professor Bloom's provocative theory of the literary relationships between the great writers and their predecessors. His most recent books include *Shakespeare: The Invention of the Human*, a 1998 National Book Award finalist, *How to Read and Why*, *Genius: A Mosaic of One Hundred Exemplary Creative Minds*, *Hamlet: Poem Unlimited*, *Where Shall Wisdom Be Found?*, and *Jesus and Yahweh: The Names Divine*. In 1999, Professor Bloom received the prestigious American Academy of Arts and Letters Gold Medal for Criticism. He has also received the International Prize of Catalonia, the Alfonso Reyes Prize of Mexico, and the Hans Christian Andersen Bicentennial Prize of Denmark.

JACK ZIPES is a professor at the University of Minnesota. He is the author of many titles, such as *Fairy Tales and the Art of Subversion*, and editor of *The Great Fairy Tale Tradition*.

STEVEN E. KAGLE has been a professor of English at Illinois State University. He is the author of *American Diary Literature 1607–1800* and other titles and the editor of several books, among them *America: Exploration and Travel*.

SUSAN SPENCER is a professor in the English department at the University of Central Oklahoma. She is a coauthor of *The Eighteenth-Century Novel*.

DIANE S. WOOD is a professor of French at Texas Tech University. She is coeditor of *Recapturing the Renaissance*.

RAFEEQ O. MCGIVERON has taught English at Lansing Community College in Lansing, Michigan. He has been published in *Extrapolation*, *Science-Fiction Studies*, *The Explicator*, and *Critique*.

ROBIN ANNE REID is a professor of English at Texas A&M University–Commerce. She is the author of *Arthur C. Clarke: A Critical Companion* as well as several articles on science fiction.

GEORGE E. CONNOR is an associate professor at Missouri State University. His research interests include American political thought and the Congress. He is coeditor of *The Constitutionalism of American States*.

JONATHAN R. ELLER is a professor of English at Indiana University. He has written introductions to several new editions of Bradbury's work. Also, he is the textual editor of *The Writings of Charles S. Peirce*, volume 6, 1886–1890.

WILLIAM F. TOUPONCE is a professor of English at Indiana University. He is the author of *Ray Bradbury and the Poetics of Reverie* and *Naming the Unnameable: Ray Bradbury and the Fantastic After Freud*, among other works.

Bibliography

Aggelis, Steven L., ed. *Conversations with Ray Bradbury.* Jackson: University Press of Mississippi, 2004.

Benford, Gregory, and George Zebrowski , ed. *Skylife: Space Habitats in Story and Science.* New York: Harcourt, 2000.

Bloom, Harold, ed. *Ray Bradbury.* Philadelphia: Chelsea House, 2001.

Bluestone, George. "Three Seasons with *Fahrenheit 451.*" *Sacred Heart University Review* 6, nos. 1–2 (Fall–Spring 1985–1986), 3–19.

Bould, Mark. "Burning Too: Consuming *Fahrenheit 451*: Essays and Studies 2005." In *Literature and the Visual Media*, edited by David Seed, 96–122. Cambridge, England: Brewer, for the English Association, 2005.

Bradbury, Ray. *Zen in the Art of Writing.* Santa Barbara, Calif.: Joshua Odell Editions, 1994.

de Koster, Katie, ed. *Readings on* "Fahrenheit 451." San Diego, Calif.: Greenhaven, 2000.

Donaldson, Wendy C. "Heroism Defined and Mentors Divided: Ray Bradbury's *Fahrenheit 451*: Selected Papers, 2004 Conference, Society for the Interdisciplinary Study of Social Imagery: March 2004, Colorado Springs, Colorado." In *The Image of the Hero in Literature, Media, and Society*, edited by Will Wright and Steven Kaplan, 482–486. Pueblo, Colo.: Colorado State University, 2004.

Foertsch, Jacqueline. "The Bomb Next Door: Four Postwar Alterapocalyptics." *Genre: Forms of Discourse and Culture* 30, no. 4 (Winter 1997), 333–358.

Greenberg, Martin Harry, and Joseph D. Olander, ed. *Ray Bradbury*. New York: Taplinger Publishing, 1980.

Guffey, George R. "Fahrenheit 451 and the 'Cubby-Hole Editors' of Ballantine Books." In *Coordinates: Placing Science Fiction and Fantasy*, edited by George E. Slusser, Eric S. Rabkin, and Robert Scholes, 99–106. Carbondale: Southern Illinois University Press, 1983.

Hollier, Denis. "The Death of Paper: A Radio Play." *October* 78 (Fall 1996), 3–20.

Hoskinson, Kevin. "*The Martian Chronicles* and *Fahrenheit 451*: Ray Bradbury's Cold War Novels." *Extrapolation* 36, no. 4 (Winter 1995), 345–359.

Huntington, John. *The Logic of Fantasy: H. G. Wells and Science Fiction*. New York: Columbia University Press, 1982.

Johnson, Wayne L. *Ray Bradbury*. New York: F. Ungar, 1980.

Kagle, Steven E. "Homage to Melville: Ray Bradbury and the Nineteenth-Century American Romance." In *The Celebration of the Fantastic: Selected Papers from the Tenth Anniversary International Conference on the Fantastic in the Arts*, edited by Donald E. Morse, Marshall B. Tymn, and Csilla Bertha, 279–289. Westport, Conn.: Greenwood, 1992.

Laino, Guido. "Nature as an Alternative Space for Rebellion in Ray Bradbury's *Fahrenheit 451*." In *Literary Landscapes, Landscape in Literature*, edited by Michele Bottalico, Maria Teresa Chialant, and Eleonora Rao, 152–164. Rome, Italy: Carocci, 2007.

McGiveron, Rafeeq O. "Bradbury's *Fahrenheit 451*." *Explicator* 54, no. 3 (Spring 1996), 177–180.

———. "'Do You Know the Legend of Hercules and Antaeus?' The Wilderness in Ray Bradbury's *Fahrenheit 451*." *Extrapolation* 38, no. 2 (Summer 1997), 102–109.

———. "What 'Carried the Trick'? Mass Exploitation and the Decline of Thought in Ray Bradbury's *Fahrenheit 451*." *Extrapolation: A Journal of Science Fiction and Fantasy* 37, no. 3 (Fall 1996), 245–256.

Mogen, David. *Ray Bradbury*. Boston: Twayne, 1986.

Rønnov-Jessen, Peter. "World Classics and Nursery Rhymes: Emblems of Resistance in Ray Bradbury's *Fahrenheit 451* and George Orwell's *1984*." In *George Orwell and 1984*, edited by Michael Skovmand, 59–72. Aarhus, Denmark: Seklos, Department of English, University of Aarhus, 1984.

Seed, David. "The Flight from the Good Life: *Fahrenheit 451* in the Context of Postwar American Dystopias." *Journal of American Studies* 28, no. 2 (August 1994), 225–240.

Touponce, William F. *Ray Bradbury*. San Bernardino, Calif.: Borgo Press, 1989.

————. *Bradbury and the Poetics of Reverie: Fantasy, Science Fiction, and the Reader*. Ann Arbor, Mich.: UMI Research Press, 1984.

Weller, Sam. *The Bradbury Chronicles: The Life of Ray Bradbury*. New York: William Morrow, 2005.

Whalen, Tom. "The Consequences of Passivity: Re-Evaluating Truffaut's *Fahrenheit 451*." *Literature/Film Quarterly* 35, no. 3 (2007), 181–190.

Acknowledgments

Jack Zipes, "Mass Degradation of Humanity and Massive Contradictions in Bradbury's Vision of America in *Fahrenheit 451,*" from *No Place Else: Explorations in Utopian and Dystopian Fiction*, pp. 182–198. © 1983 by the Board of Trustees, Southern Illinois University.

Steven E. Kagle, "Homage to Melville: Ray Bradbury and the Nineteenth-Century American Romance," from *The Celebration of the Fantastic*, pp. 279–289. Copyright © 1992 by Donald E. Morse, Marshall B. Tymn, and Csilla Bertha. Reproduced with permission of Greenwood Publishing Group, Inc., Westport, CT.

Susan Spencer, "The Post-Apocalyptic Library: Oral and Literate Culture in *Fahrenheit 451* and *A Canticle for Leibowitz*," from *Extrapolation* 32, no. 4, Winter 1991, pp. 331–342. © 1991, reproduced with permission of The Kent State University Press.

Diane S. Wood, "Bradbury and Atwood: Exile as Rational Decision," 131–42 in *The Literature of Emigration and Exile*, ed. by James Whitlark and Wendell Aycock. Lubbock: Texas Tech University Press. © Texas Tech University Press, 1992 [800-832-4042]. Used with permission.

Ray Bradbury, "Burning Bright," foreword to *Fahrenheit 451*. Reprinted by permission of Don Congdon Associates, Inc. © 1993 by Ray Bradbury.

Rafeeq O. McGiveron, "'To Build a Mirror Factory': The Mirror and Self-Examination in Ray Bradbury's 'Fahrenheit 451,'" from *Critique* 39, no. 3, Spring 1998, pp. 282–287. Reprinted with permission of the Helen Dwight Reid Educational Foundation, Published by Heldref Publications, 1319 Eighteenth St., NW, Washington, DC 20036-1801. Copyright © 1998.

Robin Anne Reid, "*Fahrenheit 451* (1953)," from *Ray Bradbury: A Critical Companion*, pp. 53–62. © 2000 by Robin Anne Reid. Reproduced with permission of Greenwood Publishing Group, Inc., Westport, CT.

George E. Connor, "Spelunking with Ray Bradbury: The Allegory of the Cave in *Fahrenheit 451*," from *Extrapolation* 45, no. 4, Winter 2004, pp. 408–418. © 20004 by the University of Texas at Brownsville and Texas Southmost College.

Jonathan R. Eller and William F. Touponce, "The Simulacrum of Carnival: *Fahrenheit 451*," from *Ray Bradbury: The Life of Fiction*, pp. 186–207. © 2004, reproduced with permission of The Kent State University Press.

Index